The Muslims of Bosnia-Herzegovina

HARVARD MIDDLE EASTERN MONOGRAPHS

XXVIII

The Muslims of Bosnia-Herzegovina

Their Historic Development from the Middle Ages to the Dissolution of Yugoslavia

EDITED BY

Mark Pinson

with a foreword by Roy P. Mottahedeh

DISTRIBUTED FOR THE
CENTER FOR MIDDLE EASTERN STUDIES
OF HARVARD UNIVERSITY BY
HARVARD UNIVERSITY PRESS
CAMBRIDGE, MASSACHUSETTS
1994

Contents

Foreword

The Serbian mayor of Bratunac in Bosnia-Herzegovina was quoted in the *New York Times* of 22 April 1993 as saying, "We've always been here and the Muslims have only been here since the fifteenth century." After hearing similar sentiments expressed in the United States and Western Europe throughout 1992 and the beginning of 1993, I realized that the willful distortion of history revealed in this statement is unwittingly shared by many otherwise well-informed people outside the conflict in Bosnia-Herzegovina. To help remedy the situation, the Committee on Islamic Studies in the Center for Middle Eastern Studies at Harvard University convened a conference on the history of the Muslim communities of Bosnia-Herzegovina, and the papers presented there are published in this volume.

Whatever the rights and wrongs of the appalling conflict in the former Yugoslavia, there is no question that the overwhelming majority of the Muslims in Bosnia-Herzegovina are South Slavs who have lived in this area as long as the other Slavic peoples of the Balkans. The mayor's assertion that they are outsiders confirms my personal feeling that, had the population at greatest risk been Christians or Jews and not Muslims, the Western world would not have reacted to their tragedy as if they were spiritual and "ethnic" outsiders (as many Westerners, so unfortunately, perceive Muslims to be). To put it bluntly, I believe that we in the West would have awakened to the plight of the Muslims of Bosnia and Herzegovina much sooner precisely if they had not been Muslims. Whether one accepts this analysis or rejects it, this book offers the intelligent lay reader a continuous history of the Muslims of this region by highly qualified specialists. To my knowledge, we have no other such book in English.

In some cases the essays express opinions on the present crisis; all such expressions of opinion in the essays or in this preface represent the independent points of view of the authors and do not reflect the opinions of either the Committee on Islamic Studies or the Center for Middle Eastern Studies. It is a great pleasure to thank the contributors for the fine essays they produced for this volume under strict constraints of time. It is also a great pleasure to thank the director of the Center for Middle Eastern Studies, Professor William A. Graham, for his encouragement of our project. I would like to add a personal expression of thanks to Dr. Mark Pinson, who gave freely of his time to attend to the details of the conference and to edit the papers, to Dr. Habib Ladjevardi, for seeing this volume through the printing presses, and to Margaret Sevcenko for copyediting the papers. And, above all, we wish to thank the Council for the Center for Middle Eastern Studies for providing the funds that made the conference possible.

Roy P. Mottahedeh
Professor of Islamic History
Chair, Committee on Islamic Studies
Harvard University

Cambridge, Massachusetts
June 1993

Introduction

The idea for this conference originated with Professor Roy Mottahedeh, who in his capacity as chair of the Islamic Studies Committee at the Center for Middle Eastern Studies at Harvard University is continually exploring new dimensions and approaches to that field. This conference represents a new departure for the Center for Middle Eastern Studies, which until now has concerned itself with the Middle East or with Islam in certain parts of Asia and Africa but not with Europe.

Most of the current media coverage of Bosnia has focused on political and military aspects and the human tragedy of the war. Occasionally attention is paid to the cultural losses, but almost completely ignored is the Islamic dimension. There are those in the West, and even in the Arab world who until recently were unaware that Muslims reside in Bosnia-Herzegovina. Even among specialists in Islamic studies, Islam in the Balkans has been a small, largely overlooked area of study that barely surfaces in courses on Islamic history. Journalists who write longer "think pieces" on the Bosnian situation make brief excursions into the history of the area that, depending on the conscientiousness of the writer, contain more or fewer inaccuracies of fact.

One important but neglected aspect of the situation in the

Balkans is that Balkan Islam is by no means a homogeneous mass. For example, the Muslim population of Bulgaria, unlike that of the former Yugoslavia, included a large number of ethnic Turks. Some in the former Yugoslavia and adjacent lands consider Islam an alien entity that moved into the Balkans. The cry to let these aliens go home is heard from time to time. But where does this logic lead? Should the Slavs who arrived in the Balkans in the sixth and seventh centuries be returned to their Slavic homeland in northeastern Europe, all Orthodox Christians in the Balkans be sent back to Byzantium/Istanbul, or Jews divided into Ashkenazic or Sephardic groups and sent back to Germany and Poland or to Spain, respectively, with relocation administered and paid for by some as yet unborn United Nations agency? Such policies would strip the former Yugoslavia of most of its population, leaving in place only some groups such as Albanians, whose presence in the Balkans goes back furthest. The numbers indicate that Slavs, Roman Catholicism, and Orthodoxy have been in the region for somewhat over a millenium and Turks and Sephardic Jews for about half that. What is the cutoff point for legitimacy? How many years of residence does one need to be considered indigenous? The Bosnian Muslims are Slavs for whom Turkey (or any other Muslim country) is not home. Any cry of "let the Muslims go home" is meaningless; the Bosnian Muslims are home where they are.

A colleague mentioned that on a news program, a former U.S. national security adviser argued against intervening to support the Bosnian Muslims for several reasons, including the proposition that the latter do not constitute a nation. One can marshall many significant arguments for or against intervention, but this should not be one of them. The former advisor, like many other observers and commentators, is well versed in the affairs of West European nation states that have existed for centuries and in which acts of warfare against minorities have been rare in recent times (probably one of the factors contributing to the delayed responses to the Holocaust). However, some groups that have no nation-state, such as the Catalans, have vigorously asserted their rights. It may be useful to remember a Yiddish scholar's distinction between a language and a dialect: the former has as a government and an army. Rather than nationhood, a more crucial distinction in the East European context is whether the group in question has sufficient identity in the eyes of its neighbors and rulers to be perceived to be separate and to be discriminated against. When considering whether a group's concerns about threats to its survival are sufficient to warrant some kind of assistance in maintaining itself, this is a more important question than whether it has the formal trappings of statehood such as a national currency. One of the goals of this conference was to present sufficient historical material to show that this group has existed long enough to warrant serious consideration by the world.

In the modern age, divine sanctions for status or rule are in short supply. There can be no absolute justification for the situation that existed in imperial Transylvania, which had clusters of officially recognized nationalities and religions and no place in either of these for the large group that was Romanian and Orthodox. Criteria proposed now for determining which groups have "legitimate" identities are arbitrary; to pretend otherwise would be simply another instance of what Hertzen characterized as the "official lie." To import categories and criteria from one part of the world to another part often is unsuccessful. A review of some recent experiences of Western legal specialists who had little or no background in East European affairs and rushed into post-Gorbachev Eastern Europe to reform law there is instructive in this context.

For Westerners trying to thread their way through the complicated claims and counterclaims of various groups in Eastern Europe, one major obstacle is a lack of information. In some cases, the apprehension felt by one group about its survival or about the threat posed by another group may be based on an event or condition that appears to a modern Western observer so historically remote as not to be worthy of consideration. However, to the extent that the event or condition has been kept quite alive in the consciousness of a group—in its oral traditions and textbooks—it is a current psychological reality and cannot easily be dismissed as merely an arcane academic concern. When, in 1971, an elderly man in a dingy bookstore in Sofia learned that I was from the United States, his parting statement was this: "When you get back to America, please remind President Nixon that Macedonia is ours." Neither the hundreds of years that had elapsed since medieval Bulgaria controlled part of Macedonia nor the official Soviet prohibition against Bulgaria's advancing claims to Macedonia against Yugoslavia (which for decades had blocked mention of this issue in the media) had made this psychological reality less real for that man and, one must think, many of his countrymen. Such subterranean views held in the Communist period are now above ground. Accordingly, the remoteness of the medieval period on which these views may be based matters little now.

By casting some light on four hundred years of history, this conference may help correct a popular misconception on the part of many that the history of the Bosnian Muslims appears to have begun two or three years ago. For those who think that way, the almost automatic assumption is that the wishes of a group that has existed for so short a time cannot be deep rooted and need not be taken seriously. Between those outside the conflict holding such views and those inside involved in the conflict and aware of the depth of traditions, a collision course is inevitable. Outsiders holding such views, whether policy makers or average citizens whose support the policy makers attempt to mobilize, are surprised, if not angered, when insiders reject compromises that to outsiders appear to be eminently reasonable and to involve little of real substance. Understanding the strength or depth of local identities is then for the West not merely an exercise in history. We hope this volume will help put matters in a more balanced perspective.

The original idea for this conference was to produce papers for a general public of nonspecialists, nonhistorians. Contributors were not to present a detailed account of the history of Bosnian Muslims for the periods they were covering. Instead, they were to summarize and synthesize some aspects of the work done on that period and not produce pieces of original research. In keeping with this approach, the usual detailed academic apparatus of documentation was to be dispensed with. The contributors, however, as citizens of democracies with long traditions of freedom of expression, went on to follow their own formats.

For those readers who will want either to dig deeper or pursue ongoing developments, I have appended two resource lists— one of bibliographies and other listings of ongoing sources of information and the other of maps of Bosnia, both American and foreign. Descriptions of how these lists were compiled and how a reader may use these to research new materials are provided at the beginning of the appendix section.

In conclusion, it remains to thank again those Professor Mottahedeh mentioned in his foreword and add two others: the administration of RLIN for allowing the download of the map records and the staff of the Map Room at Harvard, who provided the data on the relevant maps in their collection.

Mark Pinson
Information Resources Coordinator
Center for Middle Eastern Studies
Harvard University

Cambridge, Massachusetts
June 1993

The Muslims of Bosnia-Herzegovina

ONE

The Medieval and Ottoman Roots of Modern Bosnian Society

John V. A. Fine

University of Michigan

I am honored to participate in the Harvard University Center for Middle Eastern Studies' conference on the Muslim community of Bosnia. However, since the cause for the symposium is the ongoing tragedy in that unfortunate land, I want to stress at the onset that the title of this chapter may mislead people about what is going on at present in Bosnia and actually play into the hands of chauvinist Serbs and Croats. The conflict at present is only partly an ethnic one; the government of Bosnia (though often called in the press the Muslim government) is actually the government of those who want to keep Bosnia the entity it was; it is supported by much of the urban population of all ethnic groups. Most of the Sarajevo Serbs I know are still in the city, in favor of Izetbegović's government. The present Bosnian cabinet (February 1993) contains nine Muslims, six Serbs, and five Croats. One third of the Territorial Defense Forces of Sarajevo, including its second in command, is Serb.

This chapter is dedicated to the memory of Nina Dedović, age 11, killed in the shelling of Sarajevo in May 1992.

Thus Serbs (and Croats too) are on both sides. And both Croatian and Serb chauvinists want to depict the conflict as an ethnic war—to justify their states' territorial expansion, to demean the Bosnian cause by making it seem as if it too were just one more narrow ethnic one, and also to label it ethnic Muslim to stir fears of the Turkish past and of Muslim fundamentalism.

It is also important to underline the wrongness of partitioning Bosnia between its expansionist neighbors or of transferring populations to create three states based on ethnicity. Throughout its long history (medieval, Ottoman, and modern) Bosnia has had its own distinct history and culture, and this culture has been shared by people of all its religious denominations. Its enormous medieval tombstones, for example, were built by members of all three of the Christian denominations then existing in Bosnia. Although Bosnia, of course, interacted with its Serb and Croatian neighbors, its history and culture have been its own. This distinctiveness has continued in many ways to the present and is now shared by members of all three current religious groups. This special character and common sympathy among Bosnians of all three (and if we include the Jews, four) religious backgrounds exists particularly in the cities. In fact, since World War II, 30 to 40 percent of urban marriages in Bosnia have been mixed. These urban cultured Europeans do not want partitions or ethnic cantons; their goal, even should it now be an unrealistic one, is a restored united Bosnia populated by people of all ethnic and religious backgrounds.

Moreover, for those unfamiliar with the area, it is worth stressing at the outset that the three so-called ethnic groups of Bosnia all speak the same language and have shared the same historical past. The only difference among them is religious background. And I want to stress the word *background,* for to say *religion* would give the wrong emphasis. After fifty years of a very secular and secularizing Yugoslav state, few Bosnians are deeply religious. Their ways of life are the same. Unless one notices the personal name, one may spend considerable time with a Bosnian and go away having no idea which group the Bosnian belonged to.

I

The Slavs settled in Bosnia (as well as Serbia, Croatia, and Montenegro) in the late sixth and early seventh centuries. They appeared in small tribal units but were drawn from a single Slavic confederation—the Slaveni. Thus the Bosnians come from the same Slavic base as today's Serbs and Croats. In the second quarter of the seventh century, the Croatians (who were probably of Iranian origin) invaded and asserted their overlordship over the Slavs (Slaveni) in Croatia and parts of Bosnia. In regions to the south and east of Bosnia, the Serbs (also probably Iranians) came to predominate over the Slavs there. Whether these newcomers asserted their control over all the Slavs of Bosnia is unknown; it is also impossible to determine which parts of Bosnia fell under Serbs and which parts fell under Croats. In time these later invaders were assimilated by the more numerous Slavs but provided names for the resulting population, among whom Slavic culture and language triumphed. At first the Croats and Serbs did not form single states; different leaders controlled smaller county units called *župa*s. The Byzantine emperor, Constantine Porphyrogenitus, writing in the tenth century, refers to eleven Croatian *župa*s, four of which were in the north and west of Bosnia.

In the tenth century, Bosnia was briefly part of the short-lived Serbian state of Časlav; after Časlav died in battle in about 960, much of it was briefly incorporated into the Croatian state of Kresimir II; soon thereafter in about 997 Samuel of Bulgaria marched through Bosnia and may well have asserted his overlordship over part of it. After the Byzantines defeated Samuel and annexed Bulgaria in 1018, Byzantium asserted its suzerainty over Bosnia; this lasted until later in the century, when some of Bosnia was incorporated into Croatia and some into Duklja (basically modern Montenegro). The Bosnian parts of Duklja seem to have seceded from Duklja in about 1101; soon thereafter in 1137 Hungary annexed most or all of Bosnia, only to lose it to the Byzantine empire in 1167. Soon, in 1180, Hungary reasserted itself and by treaty regained its suzerainty over Bosnia, a suzerainty it claimed throughout the remainder of the Middle Ages but that was often just a nominal suzerainty. The nominal side of it is seen immediately after 1180, when Bosnia's ruler (Ban Kulin) began to assert his independence. Thus we see that prior to 1180 parts of Bosnia were briefly found in Serb or Croat units, but neither neighbor had held the Bosnians long enough to acquire their loyalty or to impose any serious claim to Bosnia.

From the ninth century Christian missions from Rome and Constantinople pushed into the Balkans; Rome won Croatia and most of Dalmatia, the Orthodox succeeded in Bulgaria, Macedonia, and eventually most of Serbia. Bosnia, lying in between, is often called a meeting ground between east and west. However, due to its mountainous terrain and poor communications it was more a no-man's land between the two worlds. By the tenth century most Bosnians were probably nominally Catholics, converted by missionaries from the Dalmatian coast. In the twelfth century Bosnia's Catholic church was under the archbishop of Dubrovnik. However, its Catholicism was primitive; Bosnians did not know Latin, and few were literate in any language. Thus surely much was wrong in their Catholicism. Bosnia's mountains encouraged localism and division into various regions (the Podrina, Bosnia [the central part], Hum, Donji kraj, etc.). Each region had its own local traditions and local nobility. These local traditions lasted throughout the Middle Ages and made the Ban of Bosnia's task of centralizing Bosnia very difficult. Periods of expansion were frequently followed by separatism. Different religious faiths dominated in different areas.

Central Bosnia, under Hungarian suzerainty, was governed by its ban; the regions to its north (but south of the Sava, so we would think of this as Bosnia today) were ruled by one or more bans of the same family also under Hungarian suzerainty. Hum (roughly modern Hercegovina) from 1168 to 1326 was separated from Bosnia under members of the Serbian royal family (the Nemanjić family). Thus this region was under Serbian rule for an extensive period of time. The northern and central regions of Bosnia, as noted, were Catholic. However, Hum (except for its coastal regions around Ston, where there were also Catholics) belonged to the Serbian Orthodox Church and had its own Orthodox bishopric. From 1219 when the Serbian Church of Serbia became autocephalous, the Bishop of Hum was subordinated to the Archbishop of Serbia.

The Hungarians, frustrated by Bosnia's assertion of independence, tried successfully to make the flaws in Bosnia's Catholicism appear as heresy, giving them an excuse to meddle and reassert their authority over Bosnia. Various ecclesiastical maneuvers failed; the Hungarians then persuaded the pope to declare a crusade, and they invaded Bosnia, warring there between 1235 and 1241. They experienced various gradual successes against stubborn resistance, until a Tatar attack on Hungary forced their withdrawal; they then got the pope to take Bosnia's Catholic church out from under the jurisdiction of the archbishop in Dubrovnik and subordinate it to a Hungarian archbishop. The Bosnians refused and drove the Hungarian-appointed bishop out of Bosnia; the official Catholic bishop of Bosnia then took up residence in Djakovo in Slavonia, where the bishopric remained throughout the Middle Ages, having no role at all in Bosnia. The Bosnians, severing ties with international Catholicism, then established their own independent church in schism with Rome, known as the Bosnian church.

Though many scholars have claimed it was a dualist, or neo-Manichean or Bogomil, church, the domestic evidence is overwhelming to show that it retained its basic Catholic theology throughout the Middle Ages.

The Bosnian state became stronger under Ban Stjepan Kotromanić, who assumed office in about 1318. He patched up his relations with Hungary, and for much of his reign was basically an ally of the Hungarian king. He expanded his state by supporting Hungary against various Croatian nobles to his north and west and taking for himself the territory to the west of his banate (the land between the Cetina and Neretva Rivers) and Završje (including Imota, Duvno, Glamoč and Livno). This territory was Catholic and had two Catholic bishoprics. The ban did not interfere with them, and they continued to function over their dioceses. After the death of King Milutin of Serbia in 1321, disorders followed among the Serbs of Serbia. As a result Kotromanić was able to conquer Hum in 1326. Here, as noted, most of the population was Orthodox. The ban did not interfere with Orthodox institutions either.

Ban Stjepan Kotromanić next supported a Franciscan mission initiated in the 1340s against alleged "heresy" in Bosnia. There had been no Catholics—at least no Catholic clergy or organization—in the center of his state for nearly a century. By 1342 the Franciscan vicariat of Bosnia was established; eventually its territory was to include all those parts of southeastern Europe where Franciscans worked. By 1385 the Franciscans had four convents in Bosnia proper; another dozen would be built before the Turkish conquest in 1463. Throughout the Middle Ages and also the Turkish period (1463–1878), excluding a handful of court chaplains, the Franciscans were the only Catholic clergy in Bosnia proper. By 1347 Stjepan Kotromanić had accepted Catholicism. From then on, all Bosnia's medieval rulers, except possibly Ostoja (1398–1404, 1409–18), would be Catholics. Under Kotromanić Bosnian mines (particularly lead and silver) were opened that paved the way for Bosnia's economic development and increased its commercial contacts with the coast. Now many merchants from Dubrovnik came; some settled, forming colonies. These coastal merchants supported the Franciscans; the commercial towns that developed in Bosnia, dominated by these coastal merchants, were Catholic in character.

What of the Bosnian church? It was tolerated by the state even after the 1340s when the Franciscan mission was established and the rulers became Catholic. The Bosnian church did not play a major role in the state and was not a state church. For most of its existence—other than occasionally allowing its hierarchs to witness charters—it had no political role. Such a role can be shown only early in the fifteenth century—particularly between 1403–05—when its leader, the *djed*, was an influential advisor at court. His influence then, besides whatever personal merits he had, was probably owing to the particular sympathy to his church of the king at the time, Ostoja. Since other rulers after the 1340s were Catholics, it is not surprising that the Bosnian church was not a major state institution. Though some scholars have argued than an alliance existed between the Bosnian church and the nobility, this too is greatly exaggerated. Connections between the church and specific noblemen can be shown for only about ten families; all these ties fall into the last seventy years of the state. For most of these nobles the services to them by the church were religious. For only a very small number is the Bosnian church found providing political or secular services (usually as diplomats or mediators of quarrels) and for only two families—the Kosače and Radenović-Pavlovići—did these ties last longer than one generation.

The Bosnian church continued to exist as a small organization in only parts of the state, until finally in 1459 under papal pressure (papal aid against the Turks was conditional on persecuting the Bosnian church) King Stefan Tomaš (1443–61) gave Bosnian churchmen (presumbaly the clergy) the choice of

conversion or exile. Most accepted Catholicism—at least nominally—which shows that their morale was poor. A minority
sought refuge in Hercegovina with Herceg Stefan. Thus the
church, a weak institution throughout its existence, was weakened further on the eve of the Ottoman conquest. It disappeared
entirely soon after the conquest, as its members were absorbed
by Islam, Orthodoxy, and Catholicism.

Many scholars have depicted the Bosnian church as dualist,
calling it neo-Manichean or Bogomil. Domestic sources about
the church (both Bosnian and Dalmatian, in particular the rich
documentation from Catholic Dubrovnik) do not suggest this.
They show that the Bosnian church, unlike the Bogomils or
Western neo-Manichees, accepted an omnipotent God, the Trin-
ity, church buildings, the cross, the cult of saints, religious art,
and at least part of the Old Testament. It is worth repeating
that Dualist Bogomils rejected all these items. Furthermore, the
cordial relations these sources depict between Bosnian churchmen and both Orthodox and Catholic clerics and officials (including those from Dubrovnik and Hungary) could not have
occurred had these Bosnians been Manichees.

We might pause now on identity labels and medieval communities: if we exclude some people on the periphery of this
expanded Bosnia (some in the north and west who might identify themselves as Croatians and some in Hum who might call
themselves Serbs or members of the Serbian church), we do not
find Bosnians calling themselves Serbs or Croats. If they wanted
a major label, they called themselves Bosnians. We cannot say
whether they conceived this term as an ethnic one or whether
it meant being a member (subject) of a Bosnian state. These
people in Bosnia also often used more local identity labels,
regional ones such as Hum, or Donji kraj.

When we turn to the geographical locations of the various
religious groups, we find Catholics to the north and west of
greater Bosnia—the areas Kotromanić annexed to his state—

and after the appearance of the Franciscans in the 1340s we begin finding some Catholics in the center of the state near the handful of Franciscan monasteries and in the commercial towns. In the latter, of course, were settled foreign Catholic merchants and technicians connected to the mines. We find Orthodox believers to the south and east, in Hum, and expanding gradually and on a small scale across the Drina into eastern Bosnia. We find the Bosnian church in the center of the state with its institutions extending east to the Drina and south into Hum. As the state expanded, the population did not move or mix much. The distribution of confessions remained as I have just described it throughout the Middle Ages. Rulers and nobles (unlike their contemporaries in most of Europe, including the nobility of Serbia and Croatia) were indifferent to religious issues. They intermarried and formed alliances across denominational lines; when it suited their worldly aims, they changed faiths easily. They made no attempt to proselytize for their own faiths or to persecute others, consciously resisting foreign (papal and Hungarian) calls to persecute. The expansion of the state did not lead to the expansion of the Bosnian church's area of operations (except for a small-scale push into Hum); and throughout this process, state expansion meant submission to the ruler by locals, who continued to run their own areas. We do not find central administrators with entourages being sent out by the ban to govern far-flung provinces.

Now to return to Bosnia in the mid-fourteenth century. Kotromanić died in 1353, to be succeeded by his teenage nephew Tvrtko I (1353–91). Kotromanić had established little state apparatus and generally left his vassals in outlying regions to administer their own lands. Thus Tvrtko lost control over much of his theoretical state, and it took time to reassemble it, which he did by the early 1360s. Having reasserted his authority over the northern lands, he then began to meddle in the feuds of the Serbian nobility to his southeast, and he was able to annex still more territory in 1374, including the Upper Drina and Lim regions. This gave him all of Hum and also most of what we now think of as the Sanjak. As a result of the acquisition of this Serbian territory and the extinction in 1371 of the Nemanjić dynasty in Serbia, to which Tvrtko belonged (for his grandfather had married the daughter of Serbia's King Stefan Dragutin Nemanjić). Tvrtko claimed the Serbian kingship. He was crowned king of Serbia and Bosnia in 1377 at Mileševo on the recently conquered Lim. From then on, the rulers of Bosnia, instead of being bans, would be kings and would bear this double title even though they held very little Serbian territory. Tvrtko then participated in a civil war over the Hungarian throne that involved many Croatian nobles; as a result he acquired more Croatian territory, including several Dalmatian cities, and by 1390 had added "Croatia and Dalmatia" to his royal title.

In the fifteenth century feuds between king and nobles became commonplace. More and more frequently the expanding Ottoman Turks involved themselves in these events, as did the Hungarians, occasionally allied to the rulers of Serbia. As a result, on occasion, a frequently victorious Hungary assigned territory on the Bosnian side of the Drina to the Serbian ruler (especially the rich silver mine of Srebrnica); when it was lost, the Bosnians refused to recognize Serbian possession of it, and many clashes occurred between Serbia and Bosnia over it. But on the whole, events in the fifteenth century involved Bosnian ruler and nobles, and the main outside actors were Turks and Hungarians. Thus details do not bear on present Serb or Croat claims.

In the 1430s the Franciscans became more active, building several new monasteries. In this period and the following decade, considerable Catholic church building occurred, and many nobles accepted Catholicism. The towns in which the Franciscans were actively operating, a high percentage of whose populations were Catholic merchants from the coast, were essentially Catholic. Despite Catholic gains, the Bosnian church—whose monasteries were chiefly rural—continued to be tolerated; the Orthodox church maintained its dominance in Hum (though the leading family of Hum supported the Bosnian church).

In the 1430s, as Ottoman pressure increased against Serbia, Serb refugees began fleeing into eastern Bosnia; thus the number of Orthodox Serbs in the region between the Drina and, say, what is now Sarajevo increased. In 1448 Stefan Vukčić Kosača of Hum, to assert his independence, dropped his title Vojvoda of Bosnia, which reflected his subordination to the Bosnian king, and took the title Herceg of Hum and the coast. The following year, he changed it to Herceg of St. Sava (a Serbian saint whose relics were at the monastery of Mileševo on the herceg's lands). Soon his lands became known as Herzegovina, a name the Turks also utilized; this name has lasted to the present. Meanwhile Ottoman pressure increased against Bosnia, and the Ottomans started picking off parts of eastern Bosnia. In 1451 the Ottomans took Vrhbosna. Vrhbosna (under its new name of Sarajevo) was to grow and become the major city in Bosnia during the Turkish period. The Ottomans conquered Bosnia in 1463; though the Hungarians attacked and briefly recovered parts of it, by 1465 for all practical purposes the Ottomans had won, though the last fortress in Herzegovina was to fall in 1481, and in Bosnia Jajce under a Hungarian garrison actually held out until 1527.

II

The Ottoman conquest brought religious changes, the most noticeable one being the large number of conversions to Islam. The old scholarly explanation for how this occurred, which was a great oversimplification, unfortunately has become widely accepted by many Bosnians today; in particular it has become the popular Muslim view of that community's own past. This view had three main ingredients:

1. The Bosnian church was Bogomil. We have already shown that this was almost certainly not the case, though probably a majority of Yugoslav scholars still hold to it.

2. The majority of Bosnians were members of the Bosnian church (or as they would put it, were Bogomils). This statement on Bosnian church membership is surely a great exaggeration.

3. At the time of the conquest the Bogomils, frustrated by Catholicism and in particular by the persecutions from king and Catholic church in the final years of the kingdom, en masse and immediately passed over to Islam. We shall now examine this final point and show that it too is wrong.

First, no conversions occurred en masse at the time of the conquest; conversions were a gradual process. Second, Bosnian churchmen converted not only to Islam but also to the two other Christian faiths. Finally, many Catholics and Orthodox also became Muslims. But this three-point theory was useful to modern Muslims, and by making them descendants of members of Medieval Bosnia's alleged dominant religion, it showed they were not newcomers and gave their community greater legitimacy. And this idea was encouraged by the Austrians after they occupied Bosnia in 1878, for the Austrians too wanted to build up the authority of the Muslim community and, by leaning on local Muslims, reduce the influence of the local Serbs—at the time the most articulate, nationally aware, and also the largest ethnic community in Bosnia.

Now I turn to the Ottoman period insofar as it relates to Serbs/Croats/Bosnians or the Orthodox/Catholics/Bosnian churchmen/Muslims. Since religious changes and events in the Ottoman period emerged from the medieval situation, I must recapitulate certain key items from the Middle Ages. Bosnia had three faiths; each existed only in particular geographical areas:

Catholics to the north, west, and from the 1340s the center (especially in towns); the Orthodox in the south and east; the Bosnian church in the center, extending east to the Drina and south along the Neretva into Hum. The Catholic and Bosnian churches were almost entirely based in monasteries. They basically had no secular clergy in Bosnia. Both Catholics and Bosnians had few churches, and the ones they had were small. They had very few clerics, and those they had were concentrated in monasteries; this meant that the few clerics they did have were clustered into a limited number of places. By 1400 there were only twenty to thirty Franciscans in the whole state (this was basically the sum total of Catholic clergy) clustered into four monasteries. By the time of the conquest (1463) there were about twelve monasteries, but it is doubtful that they had more than a total of seventy-five to eighty Franciscans spread among them. Thus large areas existed with no clergy at all.

Neither Catholics nor Bosnians had a territorial organization, such as a bishop responsible for a province or diocese. The Bosnian church had no bishops in a territorial sense at all. The Catholics did in theory, but the bishop of Bosnia lived in Slavonia and had no role in Bosnia proper. Thus many peasants probably rarely or never saw a priest, and peasants tend to be indifferent to formal religion if it is not pressed on them. The Orthodox, though they had bishops and some secular priests, also had a fairly limited number of churches and clerics in their areas. Thus no faith had a strong organization to bind its flock to the church either through faith and beliefs or a sense of community.

The Ottoman conquest brought changes in population and religion. First, the Ottomans did not categorize people by ethnicity. They did not speak of Serbs, Croats, and Bosnians but of religious groups; thus we find people recorded only under religious labels. From the start we see signs of Islamization in Bosnia, but the Muslim presence appeared on the scene gradually, slowly but steadily increasing through the late fifteenth and the sixteenth centuries. Islamization in the first stages came both from migration and settlement of Muslims from elsewhere and from conversion. In the long run conversion of locals was by far the chief source for Bosnia's Muslims. Thus the great majority of Bosnian Muslims are local Serbo-Croatian-speaking converts. At the time of the conquest there was a large-scale out-migration of Catholics who fled to still unconquered regions of Croatia and Dalmatia. They vacated lands. These were settled partly by newcomer Muslims but also by Orthodox Serbs who had started fleeing into Bosnia in the decades of Ottoman pressure on Serbia (which fell before Bosnia). Further Orthodox Serb migration into Bosnia was encouraged by the Turks after their conquest, to settle vacated lands. Some of these Orthodox or Serb migrants came not from Serbia but Herzegovina, whose soil was less good than that of Bosnia.

The most noticeable religious change was from Christianity to Islam. But when we look closer we find that Bosnia was marked by religious change in general. If we look at Bosnia and Herzegovina in 1550, we see not only many Muslims but also many Orthodox, and the Orthodox are found all across Bosnia and in many places where they were not found earlier (in medieval Bosnia the Orthodox were found only in the Drina region and Hum). By 1550 Orthodox were found throughout Bosnia. The spread of the Orthodox was partly from the migrations I have noted, but the Orthodox also gained from large numbers of conversions of Bosnian church members and Catholics to Orthodoxy.

Orthodoxy profited because it was the Christian group favored by the Ottomans. One can easily see why, when one compares the leadership of the Catholic and Orthodox churches. The Orthodox head, the patriarch of Constantinople, lived in the Ottoman capital where he was easily controlled. His whole hierarchy lived within the empire. The pope lived in

Rome, outside the empire, and was the main source for crusades against the Ottomans. The papacy had launched a crusade in 1443–44 and Pius II (1458–64) was trying—though unsuccessfully—to get a new one launched at the time of the Ottoman conquest of Bosnia. The Franciscans were seen as a potential fifth column.

We see this favoritism of the Orthodox in Ottoman court cases; some towns had one church building from the Middle Ages, a Catholic one. Newly arriving Orthodox would take over the building. The Catholics would want to keep it and complain to the Turkish judge (the *kadi*). The *kadi* regularly decided for the Orthodox. The Orthodox church received permission to collect church taxes from Christians. Their collectors demanded taxes from the Catholics too. Faced with double taxation, the Catholics would appeal to the *kadi*. The *kadi* would then tell them to pay up. Ottoman law allowed no new churches to be built and required special permission from the government to repair dilapidated ones. We find that in the sixteenth century the Orthodox in Bosnia and Herzegovina built many new churches, whereas Catholics with the greatest difficulty—and only sometimes—received permission to repair dilapidated churches. Thus there were all sorts of reasons for Catholics (or members of the small and declining Bosnian church) who wanted to stay Christian to become Orthodox. They could pay a single church tax and could attend the church building, which in many cases for the Catholics was the building they were accustomed to visit.

But in any case conversion was a large-scale and multidirectional phenomenon. We find Bosnian church members converting to Islam, Orthodoxy, and Catholicism and as a result disappearing from the scene entirely. We find Catholics greatly declining in numbers, with many emigrating but also with some converting to Islam and others to Orthodoxy. We find Orthodoxy gaining in numbers but still losing some of its members, particularly to Islam, but even a few to Catholicism. Thus changing religion was a general multidirectional phenomenon; Islam certainly won the most new converts, but Orthodoxy won many. Islam had various advantages, of course: it was the religion of the conquering state, and there were worldly advantages in lining up with the new rulers. Moreover, its worldly success seems to have been a sign of God's favor. We also note that changing religion occurred at a gradual rate, and the speed of it varied from place to place.

The Turkish cadasters or defters show both the gradualness of and variation in this process. First let us look at the Bosnian town of Lepenica over time; the defters, it should be noted, do not distinguish between Orthodox and Catholics (see table 1.1). Then examine the variation in the balance between Christians and Muslims as seen in the 1485 survey shown in table 1.2. The defters of 1528–29 provide population figures for whole area (in households) (see table 1.3). Catholic visitation reports (official church visitors) provide estimated numbers of individuals rather than households (see table 1.4). Again and again the Catholic visitors, to explain Catholic losses, stress the shortage of priests, the ignorance of existing priests, and the indifference of local bishops.

Why did so many changes in religious confession occur in Bosnia and Herzegovina and not elsewhere in the Balkans (ex-

Table 1.1 Population of Lepenica, 1468–1509

Date of survey	Christian Householders	Muslim Householders
1468	279	0
1485	329	18
1489	165	65
1509	160	393

Table 1.2   Survey of Christians and Muslims, 1485

Town	Christian Householders	Muslim Householders
Dolac	84	13
Hodidjed	35	9
Glavogodina	3	29
Doljani	19	16
Butmir	21	14
Otes	3	17
Presejenica	38	39

Table 1.3   Population Figures, 1528–29

Region	Christian Households	Muslim Households
Sanjak of Bosnia	19,619	16,935
Sanjak of Zvornik	13,112	2,654
Sanjak of Herzegovina	9,588	7,077

cluding Albania)? The reason, I suggest, is not hard to find and has nothing to do with the content of beliefs of the former Bosnian church, even though such a view is commonly advanced. The fact is that by and large the Bosnians had never been strong Christians. If one looks at Serbia, Croatia, Bulgaria, and Greece, one finds well-organized state churches, with large and thriving monasteries, and an active episcopal structure, commanding considerable loyalty. One also finds that in each of these areas one church organization existed without rivals, linked closely to the state or the nobility. In Bosnia, instead of having a single well-organized church as elsewhere in the Bal-

Table 1.4   Catholic Visitation Reports, 1624–1809

Date	Name	Muslims	Catholics	Orthodox
1624	Masarecci	900,000	300,000	150,000 (his estimate, just Bosnia, minus Herzegovina)
1626	Georgijevich	Less than Christians combined	250,000	More than Catholics (he includes Herzegovina)
1655	Maravich	Majority are Muslims	73,000	Gives no figure
1809	French consul	600,000	120,000	500,000

kans, there existed three rival organizations, all of which were weak. No church in Bosnia or Herzegovina had ever had a strong territorial organization, and all three were very short of priests. Moreover, all the discovered church buildings from Bosnia's Middle Ages were small, too small to accommodate congregations of any size. This suggests the nobles, who presumably erected them, built them as family chapels and did not expect the local peasant population to attend. Thus even those who lived near a church building may rarely or even never have attended it. Few Christians were deeply attached to any Christian church or religious community, whether through belief or through sense of community.

After 1463 Islam—a dynamic, well-preached new religion—appeared. It had the advantages of being the religion of the conquering state, which gave its members worldly advantages. In a locality where Christianity was poorly organized and generally ineffectively preached, it is not surprising to find people without strong religious attachment accepting a new faith. Since the Bosnians had long been shaky Christians, who had dealt with the Turks for half a century before the conquest, they had no strong prejudices against Islam as people from most other

Christian lands had. Moreover, religious motives may not have predominated in leading people to accept the new faith. Finally, acceptance is a better word than conversion to describe what occurred in Bosnia. Probably few Bosnians in accepting Islam underwent any deep changes in patterns of thought or way of life. Most of those who became Muslims probably continued to live as they always had, retaining most of their domestic customs and many Christian practices. They adopted a few Islamic practices, which would quickly acquire great symbolic value and would soon come to be viewed as the essentials of Islam.

III

We have seen that in the seventh century, after the Serb and Croat migrations, the dividing line between the two groups fell somewhere in Bosnia. It is not clear where the line fell, or which group—if either—stood over a larger number of Slavs in Bosnia or a larger area in Bosnia. More important, the bulk of the population of the whole broad area came from the initial Slavic migrations that preceded the arrival of the smaller number of Serbs and Croats. This Slavic component came from a single Slavic group, the Slaveni. Thus the Slavic base of the Serbs, Croats, and Bosnians is the same. In the Middle Ages the Bosnians called themselves Bosnians or used even more local (county, regional) names. In the Middle Ages there was no question of Bosnians being Serbs or Croats. The Ottomans conquered Bosnia and Herzegovina and categorized people not by ethnic labels but by religious ones—Muslims, Orthodox, and Catholics. In the Ottoman period there also occurred large-scale migrations and multidirectional conversions. Finally, in the nineteenth century, and particularly under the Austrian occupation, which began in 1878, nationalism appeared on the scene, and the nationalists taught that if one is a Catholic, one is a Croat; if one is Orthodox one is a Serb. But in terms of the origins of these Bosnian Catholics and Orthodox, this was nonsense. The population was greatly mixed (a result of the various migrations and many conversions). No one could say if an Orthodox was descended from a medieval Orthodox or a medieval Catholic or Bosnian churchman. Moreover, the terms *Serb* and *Croat* had no earlier relevance to the area's population. The terms were meaningless for Bosnia until Bosnians—as they unfortunately did—began to take on and feel such identities in the nineteenth century. But even though they assumed them, we must realize that these identities date only from the nineteenth century. Some Croatians, pointing to the late spread of the Orthodox, with and after the Ottoman conquest, try to make themselves (and the Muslims) the indigenous population and argue that the Orthodox are late-comers. This is partially true since many Orthodox did migrate into Bosnia late (in the fifteenth and sixteenth centuries). However, throughout the Middle Ages there was an Orthodox population in Hum/Herzegovina and also along the Bosnia side of the Drina. Moreover, many of the Orthodox in Bosnia are descended from medieval Bosnians who converted to Orthodoxy.

Thus any ethnic label used in modern Bosnia that its adherents try to link to any time prior to the nineteenth century (when these labels were taken on for the first time) is out of place. Though many Bosnian families have lived in Bosnia for centuries, their development into Serbs and Croats is a nineteenth-century phenomenon, an entirely new identity taken on then. If we want a historical label, then the term *Bosnian* would make more sense; at least that was the name of their medieval state and their Ottoman province and a label many medieval Bosnians really used. But neither the Serbs nor the Croats, though they have won some Bosnians over to these cross-the-border names, have any serious historical claims to Bosnia. The only recent time the Croatians administered Bosnia was the Ustasha state during World War II, which, owing to its vicious ethnic cleansing, I am sure every Bosnian would like to forget. Recently the Serbs have never controlled Bosnia—unless one wants to claim, as there are grounds for, that interwar Yugoslavia was in fact a greater Serbia. But that period was not one Bosnians would feel nostalgic for. And if what is going on now is an indication of what Serb rule in Bosnia means, marked by Ustasha-like ethnic cleansing, then it is clear that no sensible Bosnian would want their rule either.

Finally, though newspapers speak now of Serbs against Bosnians (or Muslims), it is worth stressing that this is a dreadful and misleading distortion. The attackers and besiegers make up only some of the Serbs of Bosnia. For example, as noted in my introduction, many, if not most, of the Serbs of Sarajevo are still in the city, supporting the Bosnian government and along with Sarajevo's Muslims and Croats dying from Serbian shelling. Thus, people from all the so-called ethnic groups in Sarajevo reject these narrow chauvinistic labels and feel themselves to be simply Sarajlije (people of Sarajevo) or Bosnians. This common Bosnian identity is seen in the vast number of mixed marriages since the war. Thus, the Bosnian cause is not simply a Muslim cause but a cause that includes all three nationalities, and it includes Bosnia's Serbs and Croats along with Muslims. Yugoslavs of all ethnic groups should see that the true interest of their respective nationalities is represented by the Bosnian cause, that rises above the divisive chauvinism. The cause of Serbs and Croats is not represented by the ethnic militias running around Bosnia and Herzegovina claiming to speak for their respective peoples. The true Serbian cause is that of the Bosnians. Serbs and Croats must reject their chauvinistic leaders and return to the spirit of *bratstvo-jedinstvo* (brotherhood and unity) that is still practiced by the Sarajlije in their present agony. This was Yugoslavia's salvation fifty years ago, and it still could be today.

TWO

Bosnia Under Ottoman Rule, 1463–1800

Colin Heywood

University of London

Historians, more than most people, know that cultures and civilizations can be overwhelmed and disappear in tragic, brutal, and sometimes unexpected circumstances. This professional proximity to the negative aspects of power has sometimes rendered them suspect in the eyes of the world (Canetti, 1971, 434).[1] The ancient atrocity is transformed into the learned footnote: this, after all, is what has been described as the pattern of history. But it is rare, at least in the history of the last half century, for a people and a culture based on a continent ostensibly at peace to be destroyed in the full view of the world and with the apparent complicity of the unelected functionaries who purport to represent the people of the world in its tragically misnamed global forum.

In the present circumstances of unalleviated tragedy and outrage, I dedicate this chapter to my fellow Ottomanists of the University and the Oriental Institute of Sarajevo and of the other libraries, institutes, and archives of Bosnia and Herzegovina—victims all, personal and institutional, of an unmitigated barbarism of the flesh and the spirit. For more than forty years they and their institutes were among our leaders, pioneers in the patient reconstruction of an Ottoman past that contributed relevance and meaning to the entire field. Now the scholars are scattered and their fate unknown. Their libraries and archives, containing the records of half a millennium of history, have been destroyed. May the defter of their achievements never be closed and may the infamy of those who brought this about never be forgotten.

I

Where, then, to begin? The history of Bosnia and Herzegovina in the first 350 years of Ottoman rule is a difficult, contentious, and still not fully articulated subject. There were domination and conquest; conversion, migration, and revolt; economic growth and decline, intermittent conflict, and deep-seated social transformation; and, to a considerable extent, cultural continuity. At the conclusion of a long chapter (22) that he devotes to the campaign undertaken by Sultan Meḥmed II in 1463 that brought about the definitive Ottoman conquest of much of Bosnia and Herzegovina, the Ottoman historian Tursun Beg, who had taken part in the campaign in the entourage of his patron, the Grand Vizier Maḥmūd Pasha, remarks:

> All in all, in this blessed campaign, four[2] lands (*vilāyet*) were conquered and incorporated [into the empire]: a provincial governor (*sancak-begi*)[3] and judges (*kadılar*) were appointed; commissioners (*emīnler*) were placed in charge of the mining operations, and the canonically lawful poll-tax (*cizye-i šerʿī*) was levied on the [non-Muslim] subject population (*re'āyā*). From this auspicious campaign, [the sultan] came [again] to Istanbul, the Abode of Government, with immeasurable booty, and riches without end.[4]

The Bosnian campaign of 1463 constituted a textbook example of Ottoman methods of conquest: brilliantly organized, rapidly concluded, and successful in both its military and political objectives. The Bosnians, lulled into a false sense of security by the granting of a spurious fifteen-year truce, were kept unaware of the sultan's intentions.[5] The Ottoman army with the Sultan at its head entered central Bosnia and made for the strong fortress at Bobovać (Bobovča), which, according to one version of events, had already been taken by the *akıncı* advance guard. The sultan advanced to Travnik, where he established his camp. Visoko and a large number of other fortresses surrendered, for the most part without a struggle. The districts that they had controlled became the centers of Ottoman provinces, in which the infidels paid *cizye* (Tursun Beg, 1977, 123).

The unchanging nature of warfare in Bosnia is graphically illustrated by Tursun Beg's (1977, 123) account of the guerrilla-type resistance from the Bosnian side encountered by the Ottomans and the sultan's response to it:

> Some of the enemy who were determined to keep up the resistance ('*işyān*) set ambushes from hideouts (*becene*)[6] in inaccessible places (*şarp yerler*) in the mountains. As the sultan [at the head of the main army] advanced along the vertiginous mountain paths (*nerdübān-şekl yol*) he would stop from time to time and order Maḥmūd Pasha or one of the other *begs* to flush out the resisters. Some were smoked out; others had their water supply cut; while others were overrun in a sudden assault. Many prisoners were taken, since large crowds of civilians (*memleket ḳavmı*) had taken refuge in these hideouts.

The novelty of these proceedings—it was indeed "a strange [sort of] warfare" (*ceng-i ġarīb*), as Tursun Beg describes it—was not lost on the Ottomans. From Travnik a force under Maḥmūd Pasha was sent against the Bosnian king, Stefan Tomašević, who evacuated Jajce, fleeing first to Sokol and then to

Ključ, which surrendered after a siege. Stefan Tomašević was handed over to the sultan, who caused him to be summarily executed (Mihailović, 1979, 139). Maḥmūd Pasha then marched on Zvečaj, and its garrison also surrendered and handed over Stefan's younger brother. Shortly thereafter Jajce surrendered to Meḥmed. With Bosnia in Ottoman hands, Maḥmūd Pasha was sent against Herzegovina, much of which also passed rapidly into Ottoman hands.[7]

The Bosnian campaign of 1463 was only one among several glittering Ottoman successes in the five years between the death in 1458 of the Ottomans' great opponent, the Hungarian magnate Janos Hunyadi, and the outbreak in 1463 of the Long War with Venice and Hungary. To speak only of conquests at the expense of Christian rulers, there was in addition to the subjection of Bosnia and Herzegovina, the extinction of medieval Serbia (1459); the liquidation of the last territorial vestiges of Byzantium, in the shape of the Despotate of the Morea (1460) and the "Empire" of Trebizond (1461); the definitive reduction of Wallachia to vassal status (1462), and the end of Latin rule on Mytilene (1463).[8]

Analogously, perhaps, to Hitler's successes in 1938–41 or Stalin's *reconquista* of 1942–45, these were campaigns undertaken by a singleminded despot furnished with an ideology fit for his purpose and a military machine arguably among the most formidable of its time. Unlike the conquests of these twentieth-century *Gewaltmenschen,* those of Meḥmed II were destined to endure. The territories that comprised the empire of Trebizond still make up, *grosso modo,* a province of the Ottoman empire's most proximate successor state. Ottoman rule on Mytilene lasted until 1913; in the Morea until 1831. A Serbian state—but much changed—reemerged into the light of history only at the beginning of the nineteenth century, while Bosnia remained a de jure Ottoman possession until 1908. De facto, from 1878 to 1918, it was under Habsburg control; later, after the demise of the old empires, it found new political masters but (unlike Trebizond) not a largely new population. The legal provisions for "ethnic cleansing" in the Treaty of Lausanne (echoes in an age of nationalism, it must be said, of Ottoman, Byzantine, and Roman practice to look no further afield and no further back in time, and we may now with hindsight recognize the phenomenon) were limited at the time to elements in the population of Greece and Turkey. Less legal "ethnic cleansing," when accompanied by forced deportation and systematic terror, has subsequently found many imitators. This is perhaps the main element in the present tragedy, as Bosnia—still "post-Ottoman" in its structure and society but reemergent as a state after 530 years—has found to its cost. To suggest what, if it exists, may be accounted the pre-nineteenth-century Ottoman component of this late-twentieth-century tragedy is the purpose of this chapter.

II

What was the Ottoman view of the Bosnia of 1463 that Tursun Beg had come to know in the course of a lengthy campaign?[9] "The country of Bosnia is a broad-spreading land (*bir memleket-i vesī*')," he wrote from the perspective of retirement a quarter of a century later, "the greater part of it is mountainous, with lofty peaks and impregnable castles and with mines of gold and silver." Tursun Beg (1977, 121–22) goes on to expatiate in flowery terms on the delights of its climate and the consequent charms of its youths and maidens when taken as slaves. His colleague Isḥāḳ Pasha, if we are to believe Konstantin Mihailović (1979, 137), was more concerned with the practicalities of domination and conquest:

Let us grant [the king of Bosnia, through his envoys] a truce for fifteen years, and immediately, without delay, we will march after them. And otherwise we would not be able to conquer Bosnia, for it is a mountainous land, and besides [the king] will have the Hungarian king for help, and the Croats, and other rulers, and he will take measures so that then we will be able to do nothing against him.

How had the conquest come about? To speak as an Ottoman historian looking at Bosnia in the Ottoman period, rather than as Bosnian specialist observing the Ottoman period of Bosnian history, one must begin with the policies of Meḥmed II. The seizure of Constantinople in 1453 provided a symbol, sanctified by more than a millennium of association, and a focus for Meḥmed's imperial ambitions; a formidable army and the latest developments in military technology provided the means; and Meḥmed's own relentless energy and overwhelming ambition to found an Islamic empire to rival that of the Caesars provided the motivation for a program of aggressive warfare that no contemporary state between the Danube and the Taurus was able long to withstand. Certainly the fragmented and divided collection of lordships that was late medieval Bosnia, caught between the Hungarian anvil and the Ottoman hammer, as John Fine has shown (1987, 453 ff.), was in no position to resist the Ottoman onslaught.

The political reasons adduced by contemporary Ottoman historians for Meḥmed's decision to subjugate Bosnia seem to have their origin in Ottoman displeasure at the marriage in 1459 of Stefan Tomašević to Elena, the daughter of the Serbian Despot Lazar Branković (1456–58).[10] Tursun Beg (1977, 122) puts it that Stefan Tomašević "paid *cizye* to the Imperial Treasury and was in a treaty relationship (*nisbet-i 'ahdī*) with the Porte"; nonetheless, "finding himself, through marriage with the daughter of the decrepit [former] despot, on the throne of that ill-starred one, he laid illegitimate claim to the fortress of Semendire, saying 'it is the property of the Despot's daughter,' [an act] which occasioned the postponement of its conquest [by the Ottomans]." These developments took place, of course, during the reign of Tomaš Stefan, but Tursun Beg (1977, 122) adds that Stefan Tomašević also "manifested a number of other violations of his engagements [to the Sultan]," perhaps a veiled reference to the fact that, after his accession to the Bosnian throne in 1461, he immediately stopped the payment of tribute to Meḥmed II.[11] In addition, Tursun Beg observes disapprovingly that "the evil-doing unfortunate" became king by killing his father—a statement that, unlike his refusal to pay tribute, appears to be unsubstantiated by other sources.[12]

What do we know of Ottoman Bosnia in the critical and formative period of little more than a half century between its conquest and the accession of Süleymān the Magnificent? How far did the process of Ottomanization—indissolubly linked with the vexed question of Islamization—in the Bosnian lands parallel or differ from developments in other lands conquered for Islam at the same time? How far was Bosnia typical; or how far was it already becoming in this period what has often been claimed for it—a special case?

It must be said that for Bosnia, as for any part of the Ottoman empire in this period and for long into the sixteenth century, our knowledge is patchy. Certainly, as both Tursun Beg (1977, 128) and his contemporary, the Genoese man of affairs and adviser to Murād II and Meḥmed II, Iacopo de Promontorio-de Campis (Babinger, 1956, 52–53) inform us, *sancak-begi*s were installed in the newly conquered provinces, and kadis were appointed to administer Islamic law in the newly established sharia courts. Some documents have survived (or had survived until recently), and we know the names of the earliest provincial governors and of some of the kadis. But of administrative or legal records on a large scale we have, for a century or so to come, nothing, with the significant exception of the so-called *taḥrīr defterleri,* the provincial surveys of taxable resources that were undertaken by the Ottomans in the aftermath of conquest and thereafter at irregular intervals until (in the main) the latter part of the sixteenth century.[13] Once conquest was achieved, the Ottoman court chronicles have on occasion a great deal to say on the subject of Bosnia.[14]

Bosnia at the time of the 1463 campaign was divided into two major parts, the "king's lands," i.e., Bosnia proper, and "the duke's lands," i.e., Herzegovina; in their usual conservative fashion, this division was retained by the Ottomans.[15] The "Capitano [i.e., *sancak-begi*] di Boxina Regno" held what is defined as the "realm" (*Reame*) of Bosnia "with divers provinces" (*prouincie*, presumably the former counties) (Fine, 1987): of these, the *sancak-begi* held twelve, presumably the totality, and received an annual income of 5,000 *ducati* from a region described still, around 1477, as being "per la magior parte destructe." In war Bosnia furnished 900 men with twenty-five "*barde*" and what is described as "good equipment" (*bone regalie*). The *sancak-begi* of what Iacoipo describes as "l'altra Boxina," i.e., Herzegovina,[16] received an annual income of 4,000 *ducati*,[17] Herzegovina, and furnished 600 men for campaign, all cavalry, armed and equipped as the men from Bosnia (Babinger, 1956, 52–53). Professor Hans Georg Majer (1982, 40–63) has already shown in an important article that the fiscal breakdown of the sultan's revenue and expenditure provided by Iacopo (Babinger, 1956, 62–72) is in fact the translation of an Ottoman "budget," most probably for A.H. 881 (which began 26 April 1476) (Majer, 1982, 49). It is perhaps worth suggesting in this context that Iacopo's statistical account of the Ottoman provinces and the military forces that they supported[18] may also derive directly from an Ottoman administrative source. The geographical extent and the administrative bases of Ottoman rule in Bosnia a quarter century after the campaign of 1463 can also be reconstructed on the basis of the summaries of *cizye* (poll-tax) revenues for 894/1488–89, published by Barkan (1964, tables 21–24, pp. 60–65, see map 1). The tripartite division into (1) the old "king's lands," still denominated as being "in the province of the King of Bosnia" (*der vilāyet-i Kıral-i Bosna*) (Barkan, 1964, table 22, pp. 61–62);[19] (2a) the province of Popoviče together with other places in central Bosnia, including the district (*nāhiye*) of Sarāy-ovası [scil Sarajevo] (Barkan, 1964, table 23, pp. 62–63),[20] and (2b) the combined territories of the former autonomous fiefdoms in eastern Bosnia of the Pavlović and the Kovačević (*vilāyet-i Pavlo ve Kovač*) (Barkan, 1964, table 21, pp. 60–61),[21] both denominated as "in the province of Bosnia" tout court; and (3) the vilāyet of Hersek, divided into *nāhiyes*, not into [sub-]vilāyets as in Bosnia (Barkan, 1964, table 24, pp. 64–65).

The early postconquest feudal revenues accruing to the *sancak-begi*s of Bosnia and Herzegovina have already been mentioned. The detailed *cizye* revenues for a decade or so later as published by Barkan may be compared with the gross figure for Bosnia and Herzegovina[23] provided by the contemporary Italian translation of another lost Ottoman budget of the late fifteenth century, extracts of the "intrade del signor turcho de la Grexia, 1490" from which were published at the beginning of the century by Iorga[24] (see table 2.1). There are obviously problems here: the 1490 figures are consistently on the order of 40 percent of those for 894/1488–89. Similar problems arise in any attempt to evaluate the population figures that may be extrapolated from these statistics.

III

To move to the sixteenth century is to confront a different picture, one that certainly begins to develop within fifty years of the conquest and to achieve its classic forms in the course of the third and fourth decades. Most significant in this period is a development that was not unique to Bosnia but that was

Table 2.1   Cizye Revenues for Bosnia 1488/9 and '1490'

| | | Revenues for: | |
		1488–9	'1490'*
(1) *Vilayet-i Kıral-i Bosna*		366,788	
(2) *Vilāyet-i Bosna*			
(a) *Vilāyet-i Popviče*, etc.	184,142		
(b) *Vilāyet-i Pavlo ve Kovač*	340,446	524,988	
[Bosnia total]		891,776	400,000
(3) *Vilāyet-i Hersek*		670,819	320,000
[Bosnia and Herzegovina total]		1,562,595	720,000

*(Recomputed from *ducat* to *akçe* at a nominal rate of 1:40)

manifested there to a high degree: the phenomenon of rapid urban growth linked to the equally significant phenomenon of Islamization. Inalcık's (1978, 78) observation, based on Barkan's lists, that in the early sixteenth century "some" cities and towns in the Balkans had a population with a Muslim majority, while the surrounding rural areas had a Christian majority, would appear to have been particularly applicable to Sarajevo.[25]

The phenomenon is seen in its most developed form in the rise to regional preeminence of Sarajevo and its emergence as one of the major entrepots of Balkan trade. Many factors contributed to this: enlightened local patronage, particularly in the era of Ġāzī Ḫüsrev Beg, the *sancak-begi* of Bosnia in the 1520s and 1530s; the reversion to land routes, for greater security under the *pax Ottomanica* for the trade between the Adriatic (Dubrovnik/Ragusa, later Split) and the Bosporus, which was funneled through Sarajevo; and the emergence, in Sarajevo and also elsewhere in Bosnia and Herzegovina (especially in Mostar) of an indigenous Muslim merchant class that played a role, perhaps long underestimated in relation to the activities of Dubrovnik, in the trade between Venice or Ancona and Constantinople.

The nature of the process of Islamization in Bosnia—which forms, together with the process of urbanization to which it was linked, a major theme of sixteenth-century Bosnian social and demographic history—is a question that historians approach at their peril.[26] Latter-day demonologies and national and religious myths, together with the confusion of religious belief, linguistic affiliation, and ethnicity, have done their part in blurring the issue. But the question to be addressed here is a simple one and is to be addressed solely within the context of sixteenth-century Bosnia: how far can we speak of a Bosnian Muslim "entity" at this time, as distinct from an Ottoman or even a "Rumelian" one; by what process of indigenous conversion and regional or more long-distance migration did this entity come into existence; and to what extent was consciousness of its existence apparent to itself or to others?

The process of conversion to Islam in Bosnia, in the absence of detailed comparative studies based on the Bosna *tapu ve tahrīr defterleri*,[27] is difficult to quantify.[28] On the basis of rather unscientific calculations for the western Morava valley,[29] it would appear that in that region, among the mass of the urban population, the rate of Islamization increased rapidly from a near-zero base ca. 1475 to peak ca. 1540 and then declined quite rapidly thereafter.

Ottomanization—absorption into the Ottoman ascendancy—could occur independently of conversion, at least prior to the reign of Bāyezīd II. The existence of Christian timariots in those parts of Albania that were conquered by Murād II around 1430 was demonstrated forty years ago by Professor Inalcık (1952). A similar phenomenon in certain parts of the former empire of Trebizond, annexed by Meḥmed II in 1461, was indicated more recently by Heath Lowry (1986b) (cf. Heywood, 1988). Was the situation in Bosnia in any way different? The older view of pre–World War I historians such as Truhelka was that in the aftermath of the conquest much of the population went over to Islam, abandoning their old Bogomil allegiance and becoming, under their own lords, the ġāzīs par excellence of the northern frontier.[30] We now know that, in any meaningful sense, there was no Bogomil allegiance to be given up, and in any case, as Professor Inalcık (1954a) pointed out—again, forty years ago—in Bosnia and Herzegovina in the years after the conquest, we encounter large numbers of Christian-held *tīmārs*:—in 1469, 111 out of 467 *tīmārs* in the vilāyets of Bosna, Hersek, and Yeleč. Many of these Christian-held *tīmārs* were held in plurality, making the actual number of Christian timariots even higher than these figures suggest. In addition, almost two thirds of the Muslim-held *tīmārs* had been given to support not the "feudal" *sipāhīs* but fortress-based troops (*mustahfız*) among which, however, somewhat confusingly, were a large number of recent converts (*mühtedī*) (Inalcık, 1954a).

More visible was the process of conversion among the higher reaches of preconquest Bosnian and Herzegovinan society. The usual fate reserved for members of Christian dynasties conquered by the Ottomans was, as in the case of Bosnia, liquidation (Inalcık, 1953). Conversion, however, was another way out. A striking example is provided by the postconquest career of Stefan, the third son of the last Christian ruler of Herzegovina. Following Maḥmūd Pasha's invasion of Herzegovina, Herceg Stefan fled his domains. Later, attempting to gain favor with Meḥmed, he sent his son Stefan to serve at the Ottoman court.[31] There he converted to Islam taking the name of Aḥmed and found favor with Meḥmed II, marrying one of his daughters.[32] In the service of three successive sultans, Hersek-zāde Aḥmed Pasha rose to occupy the highest offices of state including the grand vizierate, dying of natural causes toward the end of the reign of Selīm I (Šabanović, n.d.).[33] How do we classify Hersek-zāde Aḥmed Pasha? As a Bosnian Ottoman or Ottoman Bosnian or Ottoman (by adopted culture and religion) of Bosnian origin? The latter would seem to be the most accurate classification, but should one include in this category the Islamized local lords of postconquest Bosnia, the *begs* of the *uç*, and the "feudal" *sipāhīs* of the province? The observation, made in this context some decades ago by the late Vernon Parry (1969, 50–73, esp. 53)—that "to include under the word Osmanlı . . . elements so diverse in character and origin as the *uç begleri,* the local populations of Bosnia and Albania and, in addition, the "feudal" sipāhīs is to extend the term to, and perhaps beyond, the limit of reasonable observation—still possesses some force. Nonetheless, doubts remain.

An apparent indication of a later-sixteenth-century consciousness of a Muslim Bosnian entity is provided incidentally by a recent study by Professor Kafadar (1986) of Ottoman-Venetian trade in this period, in which he makes the useful suggestion that the division, apparent in the 1590s, in the sleeping and messing arrangements at Venice in the Fondaco dei Turchi, between the "Turchi Asiatici e Costantinopolitani" and the "Turchi Bossinensi et Albanesi," reflects a division between merchants who were either Turkish-speaking or of Slavic or Albanian origin (Kafadar, 1986, 202, n. 51). How far this apparent desire for separateness was based on a consciousness of differing identity or of mutual linguistic unintelligibility between two—or three[34]—self-defining groups is a useful question to consider.

One characteristic of Bosnia that remained a constant from the approach of the Ottomans down certainly to the end of the eighteenth century was that it comprised, in large part along its northern and western borders with Hungary and Venice, a true borderland, or in Ottoman terms an *uç.* This is not the place to go into the merits of this Wittekian leitmotif for the *ġāzī* interpretation of Ottoman history, but it is perhaps worth bringing in at this point a report from the *sancak-begi* of Bosnia to the Porte, ca. 1513, which gives a vivid impression of the military realities of the frontier zone (Ménage, 1976, 43–44):

On the road leading from Ključ to Kamengrad, which are fortesses of the Pādishāh[35] lying four days' journey within enemy territory, there is a strong fortress called Sokol, which was in the hands of the infidels. They would cut the communications, so that supplies had to be taken through, with much danger, by two or three thousand men. They often attacked the supply-columns, killing many men and imprisoning others. . . .[36] When recently the supplies for the *bešlüs*[37] of Kamengrad were sent off under my officer with a force of *bešlüs* and *akincis*, the infidels set an ambush near Sokol and attacked the column. The ġāzīs fought back, and there was much fighting, but finally, under the good auspices of the Pādishāh, the infidels were defeated and scattered: some took refuge in Gölḥiṣar; some fled to Sokol. The gazis pursued them, and entered the fortress [i.e., of Sokol] before they could shut the gates. They killed some and captured others, and the fortress has been taken. On 1 Ẕī-'Ka'da [?918, i.e., 15 January 1513] a[n Ottoman] garrison was put in [to Sokol]. So I report.[38]

Bosnia's role as a frontier province was not ended but only marginally diminished by the extinction of the Hungarian kingdom following the Ottoman victory at Mohács in 1526. The Hungarian *banovina* centered on Jajce was annexed, together with Slavonia, with the effect that much of the northern frontier of the vilāyet of Bosnia no longer bordered on the Dār al-Ḥarb. The northwestern salient of the province, however, continued to be encircled by what was now Habsburg-controlled Croatia, with its own military border zone;[39] lower down, southwestern Bosnia and Herzegovina continued to be fronted by Venetian territory.[40]

The spirit that animated the Ottoman borderers did not die away, and even in the mid-seventeenth century, by which time much had changed for the worse in the Ottoman state, the ethos that had vitalized the sixteenth and even the fifteenth centuries was not forgotten. The Ottoman historian Pečevī, whose grandfather had been the *alay-begi* of the Bosnian troops at the battle of Mohács (1526) and whose great-grandfather, a certain Ḳara Davūd Aġa, *siliḥdạr aga* of Meḥmed II, had been appointed under Bosnia's first *sancak-begi* Minnet-Beg-oġlu Meḥmed Beg as *alay-begi* of the newly conquered province more than sixty years earlier, could reminisce in his old age (ca. 1640) about the good old days on the Bosnian *uç*:

> I frequently heard my father say [he wrote], "We did great things in Bosnia in the days of Ḳara Malḳoč Beg.[41] The ġāzīs won such booty that I am alone, with my one retainer, gained booty worth 60,000 aḳčas. Malḳoč Beg sent fully armored prisoners and [severed] heads to the Porte, with a recommendation that my father be given an increase (*teraḳḳī*) [to his *tīmār*] and I be given an "induction" [appointment] (*ibtidā'*), saying [in his report] "The *alay-begi* was solely responsible for this [successful] *ġazā*." (Pečevī, A.H. 1281–83, vol. 1, pp. 87–88).[42]

Pečevī's grandfather was given an increase of 500 aḳča per annum; his father, after further unestablished service on the Iraq campaign (1534), was granted the induction *tīmār*, which he sought. "God knows," he told his son, "that I could not have come home more happily if they had given me the whole sanjak of Bosnia (Pečevī, A.H. 1281–83, vol. 1, pp. 87–88).

The events described above took place in the high Süleymānic age. Pečevī was recounting three generations of his ancestors' deeds a century later, by which time the Ottoman empire wore a very different face. The certainties of Süleymān's era had disappeared in the general crisis of the late sixteenth and early seventeenth centuries; what had not changed, however, was the general involvement of men of Bosnian origin in the affairs of the empire. The example of the great Grand Vizier Ṣoḳollu Meḥmed Pasha (Meḥmed Sokolović), who held the highest office continuously from the last eighteen months of Süleymān's reign, throughout that of Selīm II (1566–74) and into the first years of Murād III, is perhaps the most noteworthy among many such Bosnians, the product of the *devširme,* of conversion, or of the Muslim Bosnian ascendancy.

The phenomenon continued into the seventeenth century. An interesting example—one among many from this period[43]—is furnished by the origins and career of a certain ʿOsmān Pasha, who stands out from the mass only by an accident of fate. Fleeing in the Ottoman rout from before the walls of Vienna in 1683, ʿOsmān Pasha allowed his private archive to fall as war booty into the hands of the Markgraf Herman von Baden. It was preserved long enough to attract the attention of Babinger, who published it in extenso in 1931, only twelve years before the Karlsruhe Landesbibliothek and all its contents were destroyed in an allied air raid.

ʿOsmān Pasha's career, reconstructed from local legend and from Ottoman sources, may be briefly described. His original family name was Popović, Orthodox peasant stock from Kazancı, a remote village in Herzegovina, close to the Montenegrin border. There, as the youngest of a large family, he pursued the traditional occupation of a shepherd. He is said to have run away from home to avoid punishment after his father's flock was destroyed and scattered by a wolf, and to have made his way to Sarajevo, where he converted to Islam and was taken up by the pasha, who sent him for training and instruction to Istanbul. Some time around the beginning of the reign of Ibrāhīm I (1640–48) he was taken into the palace service. The young ʿOsmān rose slowly through the ranks: by 1672 he had accumulated sufficient seniority and patronage to be made *bostancıbašı*; in 1675 he was appointed *ḳāymaḳām* of the Grand Vizier Fāżil Aḥmed Pasha; in 1677, after the latter's death he was made governor of Syria; in 1679, *beglerbegi* of Anatolia; in 1680 he was able to purchase, for 900 purses of gold, the immensely profitable governorship of Egypt (Babinger, 1931, 9–11). ʿOsmān Pasha remained in Egypt for four years, where he appears to have enjoyed an unenviable reputation (Babinger, 1931, 11–12). As governor of Egypt he commanded a contingent of 3,000 men in the ill-fated Vienna campaign of 1683 and was dismissed from office on 10 September 1683, two days before the liberation of the city and his precipitate flight to the safety of Buda. Surviving this disgrace, in December 1683 he was appointed for the second time as governor of Damascus, but after the fall of his patron and father-in-law, the ill-starred Grand Vizier Ḳara Muṣṭafā Pasha, he was appointed by the latter's sucessor to the post of *beglerbegi* of Bosnia, although it appears to be doubtful whether he ever took up the post. Early in 1684 he performed badly in the defense of the approaches to Buda and was demoted to the commonplace rank of *sancakbegi* of Požega. In 1686 he became governor of the strategically important Ottoman stronghold of Ujvár (Erlau) in northern Hungary. Ujvár fell to the Austrians in December 1687; six months before, while leading a small detachment of men from the fortress, he was surprised by an Austrian detachment and after a valiant resistance was taken and hewn to pieces (Babinger, 1931, 14–15).

ʿOsmān Pasha's was a life not untypical for its period, in its combination of obscure origins, high office, and violent end.[44] His career in the Ottoman service seems not to have brought him back officially to his native land, although a visit to his family, after he had risen to a certain level of prosperity, is attested to and appears to have resulted in his endowment in his native village of both a mosque and a small church (Babinger, 1931, 8). His brother is said to have been in the service of the church as a monk.[45]

The old traditions of the Ottoman border, one suspects, never really died out in Bosnia. What other conclusion, for example, could be drawn from an inventory of the property left by Duralıoğlu Muṣṭafā *sipāhī,* the son of ʿO<u>s</u>mān *sipāhī,* who died in the early autumn of 1801 in the village of Bugovik near Sarajevo, leaving behind a Koran, a sword, a knife, a pistol, a musket, some clothes and boots suitable for riding, mostly well-worn, some cooking pots, two old kilims that had lost their pile, a used mattress and a home-made bolster, but no fewer than eighteen horses, some with foals, for riding or burden or breeding, some farm animals and grain, and certain unspecified properties in the village of Bugovik (Nagata, 1979, 25–28).

V

To what extent, then, was Bosnia a special case, at least within the cadre of Ottoman history? The answer to this question in about 1800 would be found to lie, I suspect, somewhere between "to some extent," "at least," and "not much." The theory of the uniqueness of the Bosnian reception of Islam via a wholesale conversion from Bogomilism, together with the whole "Bogomil connection" in relation to the late medieval and early postconquest history of Bosnia, has been shown to be a misinterpretation fostered by Bosnian scholars active in the last decades of Habsburg rule.[46] A belief in the essential continuity of Bosnian history from the medieval to the Ottoman period, the ideological platform of generations of Bosnian scholars since the late nineteenth century, can no longer be held in any way tenable. The researchers of scholars such as John Fine on the late medieval Bosnian church and society, and the more recent thoroughgoing revaluation of the history (and historiography) of Ottoman Bosnia in the period covered by this chapter by Srečko Džaja (1984), makes this conclusion inescapable. To quote Džaja (1984, 223): "vom mittelalterlichen Bosnien blieb in der Osmanenzeit so gut wie nichts übrig."

Conversely, the twin processes of Islamization and urbanization, as manifested in Bosnia in the sixteenth century, do not seem to have been all that different in terms of chronology from comparable processes in, e.g., the vilāyet of Semendire/Belgrade to the east. Although a final verdict must await an intensive analysis of the largely still unpublished *taḥrīr defterleri* for Bosnia and Herzegovina,[47] nonetheless, Islamization in Bosnia does appear to have been more intensive than in many parts of the Balkans. Some sixteenth-century observers, e.g., the Austrian diplomat Benedikt Kuripešić (1530), stressed the "voluntary" nature of conversion; others, of conversion by force, again referring to the reign of Süleymān I (Džaja, 1984, 84). An early-seventeenth-century visitor to Bosnia, the Albanian Peter Masareschi, saw four basic reasons for the more intensive Islamization in Bosnia: their "heretical past," which had left them confessionally weak and capable of transferring their allegiance to Islam "per haver qualche libertà"; the example of many Bosnians who had attained high office through the *devşirme*, and as powerful men were in a position to encourage their relatives and associates to convert; a desire to escape from the burdens of taxation and other services levied on *zimmī*s ("le angherie, et tributi intolerabili"); and finally, an equally strong desire to escape the proselytizing importunities of Franciscan monks among the Orthodox population (Džaja, 1984, 84).

Even so, the phenomenon of a Slavic-speaking Muslim society would appear not to have been as uniquely Bosnian a phenomenon as it later came to be, if we accept the evidence for the use of "la Schiauona" as a *koine* across most of the lands between the Adriatic and the Bosporus, at least in the sixteenth century.[48] What was unique about Bosnia was that, as an Ottoman ancien-régime society, it survived when all—or almost all—around it fell. The Bosnian towns of Travnik, Višegrad, and Mostar and the rural societies that depended on them at the end of the eighteenth century cannot have differed greatly from, let us say, Čačak, Užice, or Požega in the same period. But the Serbian Revolt, that great outpouring of Christian peasant resentment, together with similar revolts later in the century in other parts of the Balkans and the policies of most of the Balkan successor-states down to the present day, have eliminated the urban Muslim population and the architectural monuments of much of Ottoman Rumeli in what we might now be tempted to describe as many successful applications of a policy of ethnic—and religious and cultural—cleansing: rapid, bloody and effective, leaving no traces of what had been. Bosnian society, on the other hand, survived the centralizing reforms of the Tanẓīmāt and, its inner tensions having in part at least precipitated the Eastern Crisis of 1875–78, Bosnia, like Cyprus, was physically removed from the late nineteenth-century Ottoman world into another imperial orbit, at once both alien and preservative. The significance of these nineteenth-century developments, however, together with their further working out, must be left for later chapters to elucidate.

NOTES

Author's note: Due to personal circumstances during the limited period of time that was available for preparation and revision of conference papers, this chapter is based on a relatively limited range of currently accessible sources. I have been unable to use most of the results of Bosnian scholarship during the past half century, as embodied in the *Prilozi* of the Oriental Institute, the *Anali* of the Gazi Husrev Beg Library in Sarajevo, and the monographic literature of two generations of Bosnian Ottomanists. For this enforced omission, I ask the reader's indulgence.

1. For a discussion of this and other points in the Ottoman context, see Heywood (1988, 315–45).

2. The political fragmentation of Bosnia in the last period of the medieval state is effectively illustrated by the fact that, in Ottoman eyes, this campaign achieved, in addition to the conquest of Bosnia and part of Herzegovina, the annexation of what Tursun Beg describes as the two "infidel" petty lordships (*kāfir begcü-*

gezler) of Kovač-oğlı and Pavli-oğlı, "lying between Bosnia and Dār al-Islām" Beg (1977, 128) [hereafter cited as Tursun Beg]) but in fact west of the Drina. The Bosnian voyvode Tvrtko Kovačević, the last of his line, held territory on the Drina. He surrendered to the sultan in the opening stages of the Bosnian campaign and was instantly beheaded. The Pavlović family had owned extensive lands west of the Drina. After the loss of most of their lands (including Vrh Bosna, the future Sarajevo) to the Ottomans in 1450, they became vassals of Herceg Stefan. In 1488–89, twenty-five years after the conquest, the poll tax *(cizye)* on the "unbelievers" *(gebrān)* "of the province *(vilāyet)* of Pavlo and Kovač in the province of Bosnia" was still being accounted for separately by Ottoman tax officials (Barkan, 1964, 60). For a very early (1472) Ottoman grant of vacant land *(ḫarabe yeri)* "in the former lordship *(vilāyet)* of Pavli-oğlı," made in Vrh Bosna (i.e., Sarajevo) by the *beglerbegi* of Rumeli, Ḥaṣṣ Murād Pasha, see Babinger (1952, 197–210).

3. The first *sancak-begi* of Bosnia was Meḥmed Beg Minnet-oğlu, following a period when the *uç-begi* 'Isā Beg b. Turaḫan-oğlu Isḥāḳ Beg of Skopje (Babinger); (1940, p. 78).

4. Tursun Beg, 1977, 128: "Fi'l-cümle, bu mubārek seferde dört vilāyeti fetḥ-ü-istiḫlāṣ idüb; sancak-begi ve kadılar nasb idüb; ma'denleri üzre emīnler ḳonulub; reā'yāya cizye-i šer'ī vež' olundı. Bu fetḥ-i mübīn ile ganāyim-i 'aẓāyim-i bi-nihāyet ile murāca'at buyurdı; Dāru's-salṭana Istanbul'a geldi."

5. See an anecdote related at secondhand by the other eyewitness participant in the 1463 campaign, Konstantin Mihailović, the so-called Polish Janissary (cf. Mihailović, 1979, 136–39), which attributes to Maḥmūd Pasha and the second vizier Isḥāḳ Pasha involvement in the secret formulation of a stratagem designed to lull the Bosnian envoys into a false sense of security.

6. The word *becene* raises several problems. It is patently not Turkish but has an extensive Turkish usage, at least in the fifteenth and sixteenth centuries. Murphey and Inalcık, in their version of Tursun Beg, 50, render it as "hideouts"; Redhouse, s.v., as "an ambush" (but cf. Yeni Redhouse, s.v., where it is defined for the

modern language as a provincial usage, with the meaning of "[a] deserted [place]"). The problem appears to have been expeditiously solved by Professor Ménage (1969, 200 n. 14).

7. Jajce and Ključ were taken by Hungarian forces at the end of 1463 and not regained by the Ottomans until after the battle of Mohács. Herzegovina was formed into a sanjak in 1470; the last Herzegovinan outpost of significance, the fortress of Herceg Novi, fell to the Ottomans in 1481–82.

8. See, for up-to-date surveys and interpretations of the events of these years, Imber (1991), and Inalcık (1991).

9. For an accessible survey of postconquest Bosnian history and institutions (by a Serbian historian), see the article "Bosna" (Djurdjev), 1954, 1261–75), with full bibliography to ca. 1954.

10. The chronology of these events, insofar as they concern the matter in hand, may be briefly stated: George Branković, the aged Despot of Serbia, died on 24 December 1456 and was succeeded by his youngest son, Lazar, who himself died on 20 January 1458, leaving his daughter Elena under the control of a regency under the pro-Turk voyvode Michael Andjelović (Angelos), whose brother was Tursun Beg's patron, the Grand Vizier Maḥmūd Pasha. After the fall of Michael Andjelović and the victory of the anti-Ottoman and pro-Hungarian party in Serbia, in the spring of 1458, Ottoman forces under Mahmud Pasha had occupied most of Serbia apart from Semendire itself. Elena, a puppet of the anti-Ottoman faction, was offered in marriage to Stefan Tomašević, who took command of the fortress of Smederevo and assumed the title of Despot in March 1459. He was married to Elena in the following month. On 20 June 1459 Smederevo, the last remnant of the medieval Serbian state, fell to the Ottomans. Stefan Tomašević and Elena (now known as Maria) fled to Bosnia.

11. Cf. ʿAšıkpašazāde (1929), para. 140, pp. 157–58): "Semendire being conquered, the sultan sent an envoy to the king of Bosnia, saying 'pay tribute (ḫarāc) or I shall march against you.'"

12. Cf. the observation of Pius II (cited by Fine, 1987, 584), that

Stefan, "relying on no one knows what hope," had refused tribute to the Ottomans.

13. For an overview of the *taḥrīr* defters and of the problems inseparable from their study, see the short but important note by Halasi-Kun (1986), 163–66); Heywood (1988, 322–29).

14. Cf., in particular, for the period of the Long War in Hungary (1593–1606), in which there was considerable Bosnian involvement, the chronicles of Muṣṭafā Selanikī (fl. 1565–after 1599; see Babinger (1927, 136 f.), whose *Tārīḫ* (History) covers the period 1563–99 (Selânik, 1989) and Ibrahīm Pečevī (1574–1650) (cf. Babinger, 1927 *Geschichtsschreiber*, 192 ff.), whose *Tārīḫ-i Pečevī* reaches to 1639.

15. The later administrative developments are quite complex. In the mid-sixteenth century the seat of the *sancak-begi* of Bosnia was moved from Sarajevo to Banja Luka; later, in 1580, Bosnia became an *eyālet*, comprising seven sanjaks (Bosnia, Herzegovina, Klis, Krka, Pakrać, Izvornik, and Požega; eight, with Bihać, ca. 1590; seven again by the end of the Long War [1606], after the transfer of Požega), under the overall command of a *beglerbegi*. The boundaries of Ottoman Bosnia ca. 1606 were considerably more extended than those under which Bosnia passed under Austrian control in 1878 (see Džaja, map at 41).

16. "L'altra Boxina" is further defined as "what was [belonging to] Count Stefan" (*che fu del conte Stephano*) (Babinger, 1956, 52); cf. ibid., 82: *la provincia del conte Steffano patarino*). Babinger (1956, 53 n. 1, 83 n. 1) is clearly in error in identifying the "conte Stephano/Steffano" with Stjepan Tomašević, the last king of Bosnia, executed near Jajce in May 1463 by Meḥmed II, and in his remark (ibid., 83 n. 1) that *conte* is to be understood in this context "im Sinn von Herr, Herscher, nicht etwa 'Graf'"; the "conte Steffano" is of course Herceg Stefan, Stefan Vukčić Kosača (1435–66), the eponymous founder of the duchy itself (cf. Fine, 1987, 455 ff., passim).

17. Imitations of the Venetian *ducato* were struck by the Ottomans until approximately the time of Iacopo's survey; the first Ottoman gold coinage, which replaced the pseudo-ducat, was struck

in 882/1477–78 (Majer, 1982, 46 n. 29, and the references there cited). The exchange rate between the (pseudo-)ducat and the Ottoman *akca* at this time was approximately 40:1 (in Babinger, 1956, 32, it is 44:1). The annual income of the *sancak-begi* of Bosnia ca. 1476 would therefore appear to have been in the region of 200,000 *akca*; that of his colleague in Herzegovina, 160,000 *akca*.

18. "Sommario di tutti signori capitanei, armigeri, pedestri, cerne tali quali conduce el gran Turcho andando in exercito et cosi loro armamenti" (Babinger, 1956, fols. 16r–25v, pp. 48–61).

19. The "province of the King of Bosnia" was divided into three subprovinces, equally designated by the term *vilāyet*: (1) Visoko "with Lepenica and Dubrovnik and Grac and other [places administratively] dependent on (*tābi'-i*) Saray-ovasi'; (2) "Neretva and Dolna-Rama and Iskopya"; and (3) "Ma'den-i Kiresova and Olofča and Suniče."

20. The vilayet of Popoviče also included Gradište, Lašva, and Milne(?); also in this revenue unit were certain other tax revenues for the *nāḥiye* of Saray-ovasi.

21. This vilayet was divided into four subvilayets: (1) Boğazı Yümrü [= Pale] "with Borać and Olofča," (2) Čatalca [= Prača], (3) "Višeğrad and Hortač and Dobrun and Priboy," and (4) Ivratar "with Osad."

22. The five *nāḥiyes* of Hersek were (1) Nevesinje, (2) Sokol, (3) Preboy "with Dustiče, (4) "Ma'den-i Čayniče and Birvenik," and (5) "Kukan and Poplata and Milaševa."

23. "*Cargi* [scil. *ḫarāc* = *cizye*] de Bosgne [s. ducatti 10m?] et del contte Stefano s. ducatti 8m in s., d. 18m" (Jorga, 1909, 217 n. 5). The implication is that the *cizye* revenues of Bosnia were 10,000 ducats; of Herzegovina, as stated, 8,000, making 18,000 ducats "in s[umma]."

24. Venice, Bibl. Marciana, ms. it. cl. VI, cod. 277, fols. 169v–170r (Jorga, 1909, 215 n. 9 and sqq.); cf. Babinger, 1956, 22 n. 1; Majer, 1982, 44 n. 18).

25. Sarajevo, in the early sixteenth century, appears to have been exclusively Muslim (1,024 Muslim households; no non-Muslim);

the surrounding rural area to have possessed a slight preponderance of Christian over Muslim households (ca. 19,500 to ca. 17,000). The population of Sarajevo itself has been estimated at ca. 5,500 in the decade 1520–30 and ca. 23,500 fifty years later, an increase proportionately greater than for any other Balkan town in the period.

26. For general and comparative studies on the Balkan town under Ottoman rule, see the conference papers on the subject (Moscow, 1969; Istanbul, 1973), collected in, respectively, *Studia Balcanica*, 3 (1970) and *Bulletin de l'Association internationale des études du Sud-est Européen*, 12(1) (1974). The controversial views of the Bulgarian scholar Nikolai Todorov on the comparative roles of migration and conversion in the processes of urban creation in the Ottoman Balkans are expressed in an important monograph originally published in Bulgarian (1972) and now available in an English version (Todorov, 1983; see also Todorov, 1977). With particular reference to Sarajevo, see Hadžijahić (1961) and Kissling, (1968).

27. On the Ottoman *tahrīr defterleri*, periodic surveys of the human and fixed and movable taxable resources of a province, there is both an extensive literature and wide debate among scholars on their utility. See for a traditional view, Barkan (1970, 163–71). A partial listing of the extant *tahrīr*s for Bosnia is provided by Lowry (1981, 58). The four *tahrīr* registers listed here for Bosnia (1516, 1530, 1540, 1541) and for Herzegovina (1477, for Vlachs only, 1530, and 1532) are those containing texts of the relevant Ottoman provincial law codes (*sancak kānūnnāme*s; see Djurdjev (1957); cf. also Çetin (1979, 89, 94). The study of Ottoman *tahrīr*s by Vasić (1987, 105–14), has only a descriptive function.

28. See the post-Barkan discussions initiated by Lowry (1981, 43–45; 1986); and Halasi-Kun, (1986), 163–66; further my remarks in *Byzantine and Modern Greek Studies*, (Heywood, 1988, 322–37).

29. Cf. my study (unpublished) on Islamization and urbanization in the western Morava valley (Čačak, Požega, Užice) ca. 1475-ca. 1575, which draws mainly on extracts from the *tahrīr* registers

for Semendire published (in Serbo-Croatian in 1984–86) by Ahmed S. Aličić, the conclusions of which appear to support Inalcık's hypotheses mentioned above).

30. For late statements of this view, see Parry, (1969, 53), and (even) Braudel (1973, 664)—which is not to deny the existence of the Bosnian border as a haunt par excellence of the ġāzīs in these centuries.

31. Ibn Tulun, ed. Tulum, 128: "aḫır oglını āsitān-i devlet ḫidmetine gönderüb ṭālib-i 'ināyet-ü-'afv oldı."

32. On Hersek-zāde Aḥmed Pasha, see Šabanović (n.d., 340–42).

33. Hersek-zāde Aḥmed Pasha's son, Muṣṭafa Beg, became *sancak-begi* of the Turkoman-dominated district of Boz-ok in southeast Anatolia; his grandson, Aḥmed Čelebi, was, ca. 1537–44, one of the *evlād-i ümerā* kept at the Topkapı Sarayı in attendance on the sultan (Topkapı Palace Library D.7843, para VII, published as appendix 5, pp. 314–29, by Barkan (1952)).

34. But did the "Turchi Albanesi" speak Albanian? Cf. the comment of the mid-sixteenth-century Dalmatian writer, Luigi Bassano di Zara (*Costumi e i modi particolari della vita de' Turchi* [Rome, 1545], fol. 51v [= photo-mech. rept., ed. F. Babinger] [= Texte und Wiederdrücke zur Geschichte und Landeskunde Südosteuropas und des Nahen Ostens, 1], [Monaco di Baviera, 1963]), 110: "questa lingua" [scil. "la Schiauona"] "parlano in Dalmatia, nella Soria [sic: = Servia, and not "Syria" as misidentified by Babinger], molti nella Bosna, tutti nell' Albania, nella Bulgaria minore, nella Thessaglia, nella Traccia, nel Pelloponneso, nella Vallacchia, nel confin di terra Todescha, da certi popoli chiamati Cranci, cioè Crannoli [Carniola], tutta la Polonia, la Boemia, la Rosia." For a recent discussion, with extensive bibliography, of what the author terms "le slavon serbe" as "une langue de circulation dans l'Europe du centre et du sud-est depuis le milieu du XVè siècle," and as a language employed at the court and in the chancery of the Ottoman sultans from Meḥmed II to Süleymān I, cf. Cazacu (1992, 510–28, at 511–12, and 518 n. 4).

35. I.e., fortresses in the frontier zone, not within a regularly consti-

tuted Ottoman province, and with their garrison charges and expenses met from central funds.

36. The religious ethos of the frontier is brilliantly encapsulated here. The report continues: "Near this fortress [i.e. Sokol] are the graves of many famous *subašı*s and ġāzīs, including Gurz Ilyas, Güzel Tursun, and Mu'min Ḫoca, each of which was a ġāzī of *subašı* rank leading a force of two or three hundred campaigners (*yoldaš*): they were killed near this fortress and their graves are still places of pilgrimage (*ziyāretgāh*)."

37. The *bešlü*s were auxiliary troops who received five (*beš*) aḳca a day in wages.

38. The advantages of capturing territory were not only military but also economic and ideological. The *sancak-begi*'s report continues: "Near Sokol are mines, like those of Srebrenica . . . ; they could quickly be put into production, and *would supply the wages for all the fortresses of Bosnia* [emphasis added]. To travel to the Imperial Fortresses would become easy, so that one could go from the Well-Protected Territories to Sokol with just one or two men, and then on to Ključ and Kamengrad. Thus the troops and all the *re'āyā* in that region would live in tranquillity, praying for the welfare of the Pādishāh."

39. On the Habsburg *Militärgrenze,* see Rothenberg (1960), von Preradovich (1970), and Heeresgeschichtliches Museum (1973).

40. For important indications on the relationship between war, commodity supplies, and trade during the Long War with much incidental reference to Bosnia, see Finkel Admin (1988).

41. On the notable Rumelian family of Turkish marcher lords, the Malḳočoġulları, who appear already to have held land in north Bosnia at the time of the Ottoman conquest in 1463, see Babinger (1962, 355–69).

42. The translation is based on an unpublished collection of Ottoman texts and documents kindly communicated by Professor V. L. Ménage.

43. The prosopography of Bosnia-born Muslims in the central institutions of the empire deserves a separate study. Numerous examples can be gleaned from the Ottoman chronicles: see, for

example, Efendi (1989, vol. 2, pp. 576, 790, 793), which details the case of Derviš Aǧa—"Bosnian by birth" (*kadīmī vaṭan-i aṣlihi*)—who went from being chief falconer in the palace service to appointment as *beglerbegi* of Bosnia.

44. Cf. the career of Defterdār Aḥmed Pasha, pasha of Bosnia, who played a leading role in the campaign of 1678, which led to the siege and destruction of the Cossack fortress of Čehrin (Chyhyryn) in the Ukraine, and who was eulogized by an anonymous author—possibly the Sarajevo-born *šeyḫ* Ḥasan Ḳā'imī Baba, who died in Izvornik in 1680—of a ǧazānāme devoted to the campaign (see Hajda, 1984, 33 ff.).

45. Babinger (1931, 8 n. 4) draws attention to the better-known example of Ṣoḳollu Meḥmed Pasha, who caused a church to be built at Ravanči in Bosnia for his brother, an Orthodox priest.

46. See, for a case study of Austrian attempts to interpret this and other aspects of medieval Bosnian history in romantically fanciful but politically acceptable forms, the important study by Wenzel (1987, 29–54).

47. With the apparent destruction of the extensive collection of microfilms of these and other registers from the Turkish archives preserved in the Oriental Institute in Sarajevo (and, even more disastrously, of all the primary collections of Turkish archival material in Sarajevo, Mostar, and elsewhere in Bosnia), future scholarship will depend on the accessibility or otherwise of the originals in Istanbul. One would wish here to second the observation (see *Turcica*, 20 [1988], 171) made in this context even before the onset of the present tragedy.

48. See, for the attitudes engendered among the Muslim population, the study by Murphey (1983, vol. 13, pp. 281–92). For a well-documented discussion of the cultural background to these developments in Bulgaria, see Kiel (1985), the case studies relating to monuments in Greece and Bulgaria gathered together in Kiel (1990), and the important study of Lory (1985). One of the next tasks of scholarship will be the meticulous documentation of the results of the same essentially anti-Muslim and atavistically anti-Ottoman policies now being applied in Bosnia.

REFERENCES

ʿAšjḳpašazāde. (1929). *Die Altosmanische Chronik des Ašiḳpašazāde, auf Grund mehrer neuentdeckter Handschriften von Neuem herausgegeben von Friedrich Giese*. Edited by F. Giese. Leipzig.

Babinger, F. (1927). *Die Geschichtsschreiber der Osmanen und ihre Werke*. Leipzig.

Babinger, Franz. (1931). *Das Archiv des Bosniaken Osman Pascha*. Berlin.

Babinger, Franz. (1952). *Documenta Islamica Inedita*. Berlin.

Babinger, Franz. (1956). *Die Aufzeichnungen des Genuesen Iacopo de Promontario-de Campis über den Osmanenstaat um 1475*. Bayerische Akademie der Wissenschaften, Phil-hist. Klasse, Sitzungsberichte, vol. 8 (1957). Munich.

Babinger, F. (1962). "Beiträge zur Geschichte des Geschlechtes der Malqoc-Oghlus." *Aufsätze und Abhandlungen zur Geschichte Südosteuropas und der Levante, 1*. Munich.

Babinger, F. (n.d.). "Turakhān-oghlu." *Encyclopedia of Islam*.

Barkan, Ömer Lutfî. (1952). "H.933–934/M.1527–1528, Mali yilina ait bir bütçe örnegi." *Istanbul Üniversitesi Iktisat Fakültesi Mecmuasi, 15*(2), 250–329.

Barkan, Omer. (1964). "894 [1488/1489] yili Cizyesinin Tahsilatina ait Muhasebe Bilançolari," *Belgeler: Türk Tarih Belgeleri Dergisi, 1*(1), 1–117.

Barkan, Omer. (1970). "Research on the Ottoman Surveys." In M. A. Cook (Ed.), *Studies in the Economic History of the Middle East*. London.

Beg, Tursun. (1977). *Tārīḫ-i Ebūʾl-Feth*. Edited by A. Merol Tulum. Istanbul.

Braudel, Fernand. (1973). *The Mediterranean and the Mediterranean World in the Age of Philip II*. London.

Canetti, Elias. (1971). *Crowds and Power*. New York.

Cazacu, Matei. (1992). "Projets et intrigues serbes à la cour de Soliman (1530–1540)." In Gilles Veinstein (Ed.), *Soliman le Magnifique et son temps*. Actes due Colloque de Paris, 7–10 mars 1990. Papris.

Çetin, Attila. (1979). *Başbakanlik Arşivi kilavuzu*. Istanbul.

di Zara, Luigi Bassano. (1545). *Costumi e i modi particolari della vita dé Turchi.* Rome, fol. 51v (photo-mech. rept.). Edited by F. Babinger. (Texte und Wiederdrucke zur Geschichte und Landeskunde Sudosteuropas unde des Nahan Ostens, 1. Monaco di Baviera, 1963).

Djurdjev, B. (1954). "Bosna." *Encyclopedia of Islam 2,* 1.

Djurdjev, B., et al. (Eds.). (1957). *Kanuni i Kanun-name za Bosanski, Hercegovački, Zvornicki . . . sandzak.* Sarajevo.

Džaja, Srečko M. (1984). *Konfessionalität und Nationalität Bosniens und der Herzegowina: vorempazipatorische Phase 1463–1804.* Munich.

Efendi, Selanikī Mustafā. (1989). *Tarih-i-Selaniki* (2 vols.). Edited by Mehmet Ipşirli. Istanbul.

Elezović, Gl. (1940). *Turski spomenici* (2 vols.). Belgrade.

Fine, J. (1987). *Later Medieval Balkans.*

Finkel, Caroline. (1988). *The Administration of War: The Military Campaigns in Hungary, 1593–1606.* Vienna.

Hadžijahić, M. (1961). "Die priviligierten Städte zur Zeit des osmanischen Feudalismus." *Sudost-Forschungen,* 20, 130–58.

Hajda, Lubomyr A., (1984). "Two Ottoman Gazanames Concerning the Chyhyryn Campaign of 1678." Ph.D. dissertation, Harvard University.

Halasi-Kun, Tibor. (1986). "Some Notes on Ottoman 'Mufassal Defter' Studies." (Journal of Turkish Studies, 10 (Inalcik Festschrift, vol. 1), 163–66.

Heeresgeschichtliches Museum. (1973). *Die k.u.k. Militärgrenze.* Vienna.

Heywood, Colin. (1988). "Between Historical Myth and 'Mythohistory': The Limits of Ottoman History." *Byzantine and Modern Greek Studies,* 12, 315–45.

Imber, Colin. (1991). *The Ottoman Empire, 1300–1481.* Istanbul.

Inalcik, Halil. (1952). "Timariotes chrétiens en Albanie au XVè siècle." *Mitteilungen des österreichischen Staatsarchivs,* 4, 118–38.

Inalcik, Halil. (1953). "Ottoman Methods of Conquest." *Studia Islamica,* 3, 103–29.

Inalcik, Halil. (1954a). *Fatih devri üzerinde Tetkikler ve Vesikalar.* Ankara.

Inalcik, Halil. (1954b). *Hicrî 835 Tarihli Sûret-i Defter-i sancak-i Arvanid.* Ankara.

Inalcik, Halil. (1978). "Impact of the Annales School on Ottoman Studies and New Findings." *Review,* 1(3–4), 69–96.

Inalcik, Halil. (1991). "Mehemmed II." *Encyclopedia of Islam 2.*

Jorga, N. (1909). *Geschichte des osmanischen Reiches* (2 vols.). Gotha.

Kafadar, Cemal. (1986). "A Death in Venice (1575): Anatolian Muslim Merchants Trading in the Serenissima." *Journal of Turkish Studies,* 10, 191–218.

Kiel, Machiel. (1985). *Art and Society of Bulgaria in the Turkish Period.* Assen-Maastricht.

Kiel, Machiel. (1990). *Studies on the Ottoman Architecture of the Balkans.* London.

Kissling, H.-J. (1968). "Die türkische Stadt auf dem Balkan." In *Die Stadt in Südosteuropa* (72–83). Munich.

Lory, Bernard. (1985). *Le Sort de l'héritage ottoman en Bulgarie: l'example des villes bulgares, 1878–1900* (Varia Turcica, 1). Istanbul.

Lowry, Heath. (1981). "The Ottoman Liva Kanunnames Contained in the Defter-i Hakani." *Osmanli Araştirmalari: Journal of Ottoman Studies,* 2 (Istanbul), 43–74.

Lowry, Heath. (1986a). "The Ottoman Tahrir Defterleri as a Source for Social and Economic History: Pitfalls and Limitations." Paper presented at the Fourth International Congress on Turkish Economic and Social History, Munich.

Lowry, Heath. (1986b). "Privilege and Property in Ottoman Macuka in the Opening Decades of the Tourkokratia: 1461–1553." In A. Bryer and H. Lower (Eds.), *Continuity and Change in Late Byzantine and Early Ottoman Society.* Birmingham, Eng., and Washington, D.C.

Majer, Hans Georg. (1982). "Ein osmanisches Budget aus der Zeit Mehmeds des Eroberers." *Der Islam,* 59(1), 46 n. 29.

Ménage, V. L. (1969). "On the Ottoman Word Aḥriyān/Aḥiryan." *Archivum Ottomanicum,* 1, 197–200.

Ménage, V. L. (1976). "An Ottoman Manual of Provincial Correspondence." *Wiener Zeitschrift fuer die Kunde des Morgenlandes,* 68, 43–44.

Mihailović, Konstantin. (1979). *Memoirs.* Translated and edited by B. Stolz and Priscilla Soucek. Ann Arbor.

Murphey, Rhoads. (1983). "The City of Belgrade in the Early Years of Serbian Self-Rule." In A. Tietze (Ed.), *Habsburgisch-osmanische Beziehungen,* Vienna, 26.–30. September 1983 (Beihefte zu WZKM, vol. 13). Vienna.

Nagata, Yuzo. (1979). *Materials on the Bosnian Notables.* Tokyo.

Parry, V. P. (1969). "Elite Elements in the Ottoman Empire." In Rupert Wilkinson (Ed.), *Governing Elites: Studies in Training and Selection.* New York.

Pečevī, Ibrahīm. (A.H. 1281–83). *Tārīḫ-i Pečevī* (2 vols.). Uncritical ed. Istanbul.

Rothenberg, Gunther E. (1960). *The Austrian Military Border in Croatia, 1522–1747.* Urbana, Ill.

Šabanović, H. (n.d.). "Hersek-zade Ahmed Pasha." *Encyclopedia of Islam 2,* 2, 340–42.

Selâniki, Mustafa. (1989). *Tarih-i Selaniki* (2 vols.). Edited by M. Ipşirli. Istanbul.

Todorov, Nikolai. (1977). *La ville balkanique sous les Ottomanes (XV–XIXe s.).* London.

Todorov, Nikolai. (1983). *The Balkan City 1400–1900.* Seattle, Wash.

Vasić, Milan. (1987). "Die türkischen Konskriptionsbücher als Quellen fur die Geschichte Bosniens und der Herzegowina im 15. und 16. Jahrundert." In J.-L. Bacque-Grammont and E. Van Donzel (Eds.), *Comité international d'études pré-ottomanes et ottomanes.* Proceedings of the Sixth Symposium, Cambridge, 1–4 July 1984. Istanbul, Paris, Leiden.

von Preradovich, N. (1970). *Des Kaisers Grenzer: 300 Jahre Türkenabwehr.* Vienna.

Wenzel, Marian. (1987). "Bosnian History and Austro-Hungarian Policy: Some Medieval Belts, the Bogomil Romance and the King Tvrtko Graves." *Peristil (Zbornik Radova za Povijest Umjetnosti (Zagreb),* 30, 29–54.

THREE

Ottoman Bosnia, 1800 to 1878

Justin McCarthy

University of Louisville

By the beginning of the nineteenth century, Bosnia[1] was one of the least developed and most autonomous provinces of the Ottoman empire, an extreme example of the effects of two centuries of administrative decay and decentralization on the Ottoman provinces. The political history of Bosnia in the nineteenth century, at least until its occupation by Austria in 1878, was shaped by the reclamation of Ottoman authority over the province.

CHARACTERISTICS OF OTTOMAN BOSNIA

The mountainous character of Bosnia has defined its political and economic life. The Bosnian range has fourteen mountains over 2,000 meters high, and the province is mountainous or hilly throughout. Human habitation is centered in river valleys and passes between mountains and high hills. The altitudes of settlements vary considerably. Sarajevo is over 2,000 feet above sea level, Mostar less than 200 feet, İzvornik and Bihke 550 and 750 feet, respectively. Although western Herzegovina is slightly warmer than the rest, most of Bosnia is cold in winter and hot in summer. Temperatures can drop to 0 degrees Fahrenheit in winter and rise to near 90 in summer (as in the northeastern United States). Precipitation is approximately 1000 mm. in most of the province (also about the same as the eastern and middle western United States), 1500 mm. in western Herzegovina (as in Florida or Louisiana). Throughout the year, humidity averages 50–75 percent in western Herzegovina and 70–90 percent in the rest of the province. Sarajevo and Banaluka average 150 days of rainfall, Mostar 130 days, İzvornik 110, and Bihke 120. Snow covers most of the land throughout the winter.

The altitude and relatively high precipitation gives Bosnia a geographical character very different from most of the rest of the Ottoman empire. Unlike Anatolia or the Arab Middle East, Bosnia has a wealth of timber. Mountains are heavily forested, lumber abundant.

Administrative Divisions

Bosnia (Bosna in Ottoman Turkish) was organized as a separate Ottoman province under a governor in 1580 (for more on Bosnia province, see Birken, 1976). Until 1639, its capital was Banaluka. After 1700, the capital alternated between Travnik and Sarajevo. Hersek (Herzegovina), originally a separate province, was made part of Bosnia province in 1833. Early in the nineteenth century, Yenipazar was sometimes attached to Bosnia, sometimes not. It was part of Bosnia province from 1850 to 1875. A small portion of the province in the east was detached in 1833 and given to Serbia. In 1875 a Hersek province was created from the Hersek and Yenipazar sanjaks. In 1878, when Bosnia and Herzegovina were taken by the Austrians, Yenipazar was left to the Ottoman Empire.[2] It was made part of the province of Kosova. Although Yenipazar was under Ottoman administration, Austria stationed garrisons in the sanjak (Birken, 1976).

Ottoman Bosnia, Borders in 1870

Bosnia reached its greatest extent after 1830 (see the map of Bosnia in 1870). The *vilayet* (province) of Bosnia was divided into seven sanjaks, and each sanjak into *kazas* (districts) (see table 3.1). (Note that *kaza* names sometimes changed and *kazas* were sometimes divided or combined, so the *kaza* names in the table may differ slightly over the years.) The names of the administrative units commonly reflected the history and ethnic makeup of the province. Most of the names were Slavic, transliterated into Ottoman Turkish. However, some were distinctively Turkish: Saray (palace), Yenipazar (new market), Akhisar (white castle), etc.

Table 3.1 Administrative Divisions of Bosnia in 1870

Saray	İzvornik	Travnik	Bihke
Nefs-i Saray (Sarajevo)	Tuzla	Travnik	Bihke (Bihač)
Visoka (Visoko)	Balna	Yayçe (Jajce)	Novasıl (Novi)
Koniçe (Konjic)	İzvornik (Zvornik)	Akhisar (Prozor)	Uştroşça (Tržać)
Çayniçe (Čajniče)	Sireberniçe (Srebrenice)	Glamoç (Glamoč)	Konstaniçe (Kostajnica)
Vişegrad (Višegrad)	Berça (Brčka)	Ahlovna (Livno)	Maden (Stari Majdan)
Çelebi Pazar (Rogatica)	Maglay (Maglaj)		Pridor (Prijedor)
Kaladina (Kladanj)	Gradaçaç (Gradačac)		Krupa

Yenipazar	Banaluka	Hersek (Herzogovina)
Seniçe (Sjenica)	Banaluke (Banja Luka)	Mostar
Yenipazar (Novi Bazar)	Gradişka (Gradiška??)	Tirebin (Trebinje)
Taşlıca (Pljevlja)	Teşne (Tešanj)	Lubuşka (Ljubuška)
Yenivaroş (Nova Varoš)	Derbend (Derventa)	Istoiça (Stolac)
Akova (Bijelo Polje)		Foyniçe (Fojnice)
Mitroviçe (Mitrovica)		Gaçka (Gačko)
Pirepol (Prijepolje)		Nevasin (Nevesinje)
Tırgovişte (Tirgovište)		Foça (Foča)
Kolaşin (Kolašin)		Niksik (Nikšic)
Vasevik		Bileke (Bileca)

Source: *Bosna Vilâyeti Salnamesi* and Birken (1976).

Population

The population of Bosnia in Ottoman times was divided by religious affiliation, and it remains so to this day. The Ottoman millet system encouraged this division by organizing the population by religion. Each religious group traditionally provided its own schools, welfare system, courts, and other structures that in the West are usually provided by the government. Ethnic groups were not officially recognized by the Ottomans; population figures listed people by religion: "Islam" (Muslim), "Rum" (Greek Orthodox), "Latin" (Catholic), and so on. Fairly accurate statistics on the numbers of each religious group only appeared at the end of the Ottoman period, because only then did the government have the power and administrative ability to keep population registers.

The populations in table 3.2 have been adjusted for the undercount of women and young children always seen in Ottoman

Table 3.2   The Population of Bosnia Province ca. 1870

	Muslim	Orthodox	Catholic	Jewish	Non-Muslim Gypsy	Total
Saray	98,921	51,566	24,590	2,696	1,903	179,675
İzvornik	178,964	131,471	32,787	354	5,521	349,098
Travnik	122,251	70,547	65,110	441	1,850	260,199
Bihke	127,027	104,343	5,898	0	1,124	238,393
Yenipazar	147,942	85,952	0	112	2,086	236,093
Banaluka	84,061	126,288	40,554	65	1,656	252,623
Hersek	110,964	66,041	51,414	0	1,900	230,319
Total	870,128	636,208	220,353	3,669	16,041	1,746,399

Source: *1287 Bosna Vilâyeti Salnamesi.*

population statistics. They should be taken as reasonable approximations.[3] Figures are for Ottoman subjects resident in the province; they do not include nonresidents, such as Austrian, Serbian, or Montenegran subjects who were working or even living for extended periods in Bosnia.

As indicated on the map of the relative proportions of main religious groups in 1870, religious groups were scattered. The provinces with the highest proportion of Orthodox Serbs were not those along the Serbian border, as one might expect, but along the border with Croatia. Correspondingly, the Bihke sanjak, which was in northwest Bosnia and bordered Croatia on the north and west, had a smaller proportion of Catholics than any other Bosnian sanjak except Yenipazar, which had none.

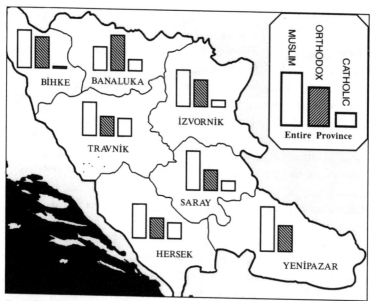

Bosnia: Relative Proportion of Main Religious Groups, 1870

Muslims, the largest of the major groups, comprised just under 50 percent of the total population.

Population was most dense in the northern districts of the province. Bihke sanjak had almost twice as many people per square mile as were in Yenipazar in the far southeast. The density of population in the central and southern sanjaks was on average more than one-third less than that of Bihke, Banaluka, and İzvornik in the north. In the absence of accurate population statistics it is not possible to tell how migration might have affected population density. However, it is likely that some Bosnians moved to the northern provinces in the course of the nineteenth century, drawn by the increase in trade that came with proximity to Austria-Hungary.

Cities

The typical Bosnian city is situated in a river valley, stretching along both sides of a river and up the sides of hills. Populations of the cities in the nineteenth century are difficult to ascertain because official Ottoman data on city size have not yet been found and because of confusion over what constituted a city. Travelers' accounts give widely varying estimates, which indicates that some included only the closest settlements while others included nearby villages that interacted economically and socially with the city. Nevertheless, it is obvious that urbanization was not far advanced in Ottoman Bosnia. The only large urban area in Bosnia was Saray (Sarajevo), the capital, with slightly more than 30,000 inhabitants in the period just before the end of Ottoman rule. It was a flourishing Muslim city; the city and surroundings (*kaza*) contained 101 congregational mosques and smaller neighborhood mosques (*mescid*), 7 religious schools (*medrese*), 9 lodges (*tekke*), for Muslim mystic orders or Sufis, and 17 tombs or shrines of holy men (*türbe*). Economically, the city was considerably better developed than any other in the province. It had more than 30 *hans* (caravan-serais, or inns with warehouses and shops), more than 1,600 shops, and a large number of mills and bakeries. The inhabitants could refresh themselves at any one of 56 coffee houses.

Sarajevo's position as main city was not based on its status as capital. It was rather the reverse: the capital was moved to Sarajevo from much smaller and less developed Travnik because Sarajevo was less traditional and more at the economic center of the province.

The form of Sarajevo was distinctly that of an Ottoman city, reflecting the culture of Islam. Streets were relatively narrow and winding. The design of houses turned inward, with gardens and outdoor living space enclosed by walls and not seen from the street. The next two largest cities, Mostar and Banaluka, each had nearly 15,000 inhabitants. Mostar, like Sarajevo, was built on what contemporary Europeans called the "Oriental design." Streets were narrow and winding. Houses were surrounded by compounds.

No other city had more than 15,000 inhabitants. In the other sanjaks, economic life was spread over a number of small towns, each with a few stores and hans, reflecting the limited commerce of the province. Crops and handicrafts were brought to small local centers to be processed. There was no economic need for large regional centers. One European traveler (Arbuthnot, 1862, 41) described the administrative centers of the Bosnian sanjaks, the largest cities in their areas, as "nothing more than large villages, with a bazaar." Most of the sanjak centers had less than 5,000 inhabitants.

The proportion of non-Muslims in cities seems to have increased beginning at least by the middle of the century. The phenomenon was observed by contemporaries and continued into the Austrian period, when the proportion of Muslims in most urban populations fell each year. In Herzegovina, for example, the Muslims comprised 59 percent of the population of

Mostar in 1879, 54 percent in 1885, and 48 percent in 1895 (Danes, 1903, 60–70). The Muslim population of the cities increased slowly, at roughly the rate of natural increase, but the Christian populations were migrating to cities and so increasing their proportion of the urban population. Contemporary European observers, when they remarked on this phenomenon, attributed it to increasing international trade and commerce, which was much more a Christian than a Muslim preserve.

Rural Areas

To those familiar with housing in the Ottoman Middle East, the feature that most set Bosnian rural houses apart was the use of wood. Where elsewhere mud (unfired) brick would have been used, for example, to construct compound or stable walls, in Bosnia wood was common. Logs and stone formed the foundations for houses, even houses that were largely constructed of mud brick. Whereas the walls of mud-brick houses elsewhere were made entirely of the brick, Bosnian mud-brick walls were made of alternating layers of brick and wood. Wooden houses, constructed of cut boards, were common. Wooden shingles or, occasionally straw, placed over beams covered pitched roofs. The hilly terrain allowed peasants to construct houses that were partially built into hillsides. Cellars are often cut into hillsides and the house constructed above them. Stables and other farm buildings were built as well as, and sometimes better than, the peasants' houses. They were constructed of the same materials as the houses and in the same fashion. Corrals were built of poles and boards.

Two-story wooden houses of a type seen in wooded areas of Anatolia and elsewhere in the Balkans were seen in Bosnia as well. As elsewhere, the ground floor often functioned as a stable or storage area and often as a kitchen. The upper stories often protruded over the lower, with wide eaves providing protection from rain and snow. While the building materials may have been different than in other areas of the rural Ottoman empire, the arrangement and use of living space within the houses were similar. Larger houses consisted of central halls from which private rooms or sitting rooms opened. The traditional separation between public rooms where friends and visitors were received and private or family rooms was retained. The main difference between Bosnian and other Ottoman houses was the presence of a kitchen in the center of the house, often in the main hall, not outside the dwelling proper, undoubtedly an innovation inspired by the cold winters. As in the Ottoman Middle East, houses were often extended to accommodate additions to the extended family. Married couples had private rooms, but other rooms were used in common.

There seems to have been little difference between Christian and Muslim housing in Bosnia. Of the structures described here, only the two-story wooden houses were almost exclusively Muslim. Muslims do seem to have constructed more walls and higher fences. Christians, of course, were the only ones to build pigsties (see Cvijić, 1956; Thurnher, 1956).[4]

The type of crops and animals on Bosnian farms varied considerably from those usually grown in the Ottoman empire. The most common cereal grain was corn (maize), an unusual primary crop anywhere in Eurasia. In the Ottoman empire as a whole, wheat production was approximately seven times corn production, but in Bosnia almost twice as much corn was produced as wheat. Barley and oats were also grown. Cattle were also more prevalent in Bosnia than elsewhere in the empire. There were almost as many head of cattle as sheep in Bosnia. In the empire as a whole, sheep outnumbered cows ten to one. The large number of cows was especially unusual in Ottoman Europe. For example, in Kosova and Manastir provinces, geographically close to Bosnia, sheep outnumbered cows twenty to one. The mountainous terrain was not the reason; other mountainous provinces of the empire also had far more sheep than cows. Therefore, the prevalence of beef in Bosnia may be a sign of a cultural difference. Goats were also plentiful, especially in the wooded highlands, where they wreaked havoc on young trees. The main export crop of Bosnia was plums and of Herzegovina, tobacco.

We know relatively little about the lives of peasants in Ottoman Bosnia, and it is difficult to describe with certainty their situation. Approximately half seem to have been freeholders—peasants who owned their own land. Their lands most often consisted of scattered small holdings that would together support an extended family. As in the rest of the Ottoman empire, the peasants did not normally own consolidated plots in which all their holdings were together. Generations of inheritance and buying and selling had left peasant families with scattered plots. Early in the nineteenth century, freehold peasants were taxed locally, and little of their payment made its way to the central government in Istanbul. As Ottoman power in the province increased, their payments went to the provincial capital and then on to Istanbul.

The other group of Bosnian cultivators were sharecroppers and serfs (kmets). Many of these were peasants who lived on lands owned by the sultan (miri lands). Some of these lands had been given by early sultans to landlords who enjoyed part of the proceeds from the harvest in return for military service and policing their districts, a system that remained in force in Bosnia long after it had virtually disappeared in the rest of the empire. Other imperial lands were distributed to tax farmers, who collected rents for the government and kept a portion for themselves. Legally, both types of landholder could be replaced at the will of the sultan when the old holder died or when a fixed term as tax farmer was over. In fact, the sultan's land often remained in the same family for many generations. Many of the holders transferred the lands into de facto private ownership in the eighteenth century, when the government was too weak to prevent them doing so. Cultivators on the imperial lands were usually tied to the land. This was partly due to imperial laws designed to protect both the cultivator and tax base, which denied the landlord the right to evict tenant farmers. In some periods, laws were passed that correspondingly denied the renters the right to leave. A primary reason cultivators remained on the land, however, must have been that there was nowhere else to go.[5]

While the majority of Muslim peasants were freeholders, the majority of Orthodox Serbian peasants were sharecroppers. The *kmet* system in Bosnia was a combination of the older pre-Ottoman system of serfdom and the Ottoman system of land tenure. Before the Ottoman conquest, Bosnian serfdom was relatively relaxed, allowing some freedom of movement of the serf. Along with feudal obligations, peasants inherited family lands and had specific rights on those lands. This fit into the Ottoman system well. Serfdom, as such, did not exist in Ottoman law, but landlords did exert considerable power over the villagers on their lands. Therefore, the traditional system of land tenure could largely continue. Many nobles converted to Islam and continued to exercise their traditional rights, which were only somewhat affected by the change to the Ottoman legal system. Other lands passed into the hands of Ottoman notables and tax farmers from elsewhere, who held the lands under Ottoman law as well, in practice becoming indistinguishable from the native Bosnian landlords who had converted to Islam.

The one radical change in land tenure came with the mass conversion of many Bosnians to Islam soon after the Ottoman conquest. Most of the new Muslims seem to have been allowed to convert their holdings into what in fact were freehold farms. Only a small percentage of Muslims were *kmets*.

The land tenure system in Bosnia was very unfavorable to

the central government. During and after the Tanzimat the Ottoman government wished to increase the taxes collected from Bosnia (see the section on Ottoman reform, below). The illegal conversion of imperial lands to private ownership and the reluctance of Bosnian landowners to forward the "sultan's share" robbed the imperial treasury. Therefore, one of the first intentions of nineteenth-century Ottoman reformers was to regularize land tenure and taxation from crops. This proved to be almost impossible. *Kmet* peasants, while they received the right to leave state-owned lands in 1848, did not receive similar rights on private lands until 1876, along with limited rights to buy their plots from landowners. The Austrians also felt this difficulty. After taking the province, they too found it impossible to abolish the *kmet* system, which remained essentially intact until after World War I.

Education

The education to be had in Bosnia was meager. Although the Ottoman empire had begun to modernize its educational system by the middle of the nineteenth century, Bosnia had taken little part in the changes. Elementry education in Bosnia was almost entirely parochial—religious schools operated by the millets. In 1875 there were only ten small modern secondary schools in the province. Students in Muslim elementary schools numbered 23,000 males and 11,000 females, in Christian and Jewish elementary schools, 3,000 males and 1,000 females, for 38,000 in total.[6] This meant that only 10 percent of the children received any schooling, and of these, an even smaller number finished the elementary course of study, which was in any case heavily weighted toward religious training.

The educational situation in the province demonstrates how peripheral Bosnia was in the Ottoman empire. The level of education in Bosnia was on a par with, or below that, of provinces in eastern Anatolia, which are usually considered very underdeveloped. The Anatolian and Balkan provinces that lay closest to Istanbul enjoyed a much higher standard of education. Student numbers at elementary schools of the type seen in Bosnia would be four times as high as in Bosnia and secondary schools much more numerous.

Transportation and Economy

Bosnia traditionally produced few manufactured goods. Only hand-woven items such as blankets and carpets had a small export trade through Dalmatia and Trieste. Manufacturing was surely not impossible. There were throughout the nineteenth century workshops that manufactured guns for the province, and other manufactured goods could obviously have been made. All of the economic problems of the Ottoman empire—such as lack of capital, low education levels, and high taxation—stood in the way of export and encouraged economic stagnation.

In addition, Bosnia manufactures and trade had a particular predicament in transportation (see map of routes in 1875). Transportation to Bosnia from other Ottoman territories was poor. There were no direct rail connections to Bosnia from Istanbul. The only rail connection to the province was the Selanik-Üskup line. Construction on this line had begun only in 1872, and by the time Austria occupied Bosnia, the line had extended to Mitroviçe on the border of Yenipazar sanjak. Transportation from that point was by horse or donkey. An indication of the speed of travel is seen in the time it took Ottoman post horses to travel from town to town (see table 3.3). Their speed can be considered an upper maximum. As Sarajevo (Saray) is only approximately 140 miles from Mitroviçe as the crow flies, it is obvious that transportation was not rapid. Of course, roads did not follow a straight line; mountainous terrain meant winding roads and they were not well

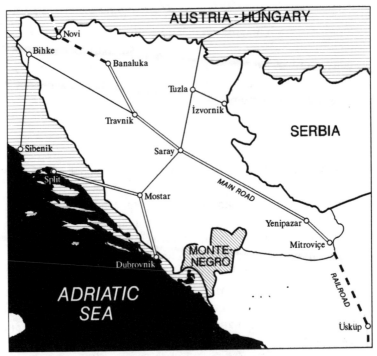

Bosnia: Main Transportation Routes, 1875

developed. The Ottomans had begun a program of constructing improved trunk roads through the Balkans, but they had not reached Bosnia by 1877. Carts were often impractical, and roads were sometimes closed in winter. Pack animals were a more usual form of conveyance. Transport of bulk cargoes to the rest of the Ottoman empire was thus uneconomical.

The transportation situation was much worse through most of the nineteenth century, when there was no railhead at Mitroviçe. Then all long-distance travel within and from Bosnia was by slow road. In all but the last years of Ottoman rule, transportation from anywhere else in the empire to Bosnia was by road or through Austrian Dalmatian ports.

Table 3.3   Travel in Bosnia

	Hours by Horse
Mitroviçe to Yenipazar	8 hours
Yenipazar to Seniçe	10 hours
Seniçe to Yenivaroş	6 hours
Yenivaroş to Pirepol	8 hours
Pirepol to Vişegrad	8 hours
Vişegrad to Çelebipazar	8 hours
Çelebipazar to Saray	8 hours
Total	56 hours

Source: 1296 Devlet *Salname*.

Long before the Austrian occupation of the province in 1878, Bosnia was in the Austro-Hungarian economic sphere. From antiquity, the natural outlet for Bosnian trade had been the Adriatic coast ports. The Sarajevo–Mostar–Ragusa/Dubrovnik road, connecting up by sea to Venice and elsewhere, was the terminus of the classical Ottoman trade route that stretched from the Bosporus to the Adriatic. In the ninteenth century the Adriatic ports were all in Austrian hands.

Road building, especially to the north, began in earnest under governors Ömer Pasha and Osman Pasha in the 1860s. The improved transportation routes all went from south to north or from the province's center to Dalmatia. Roads to Serbia were poorly developed. This may have partly been a political decision because connection between the Bosnian Serbs and Serbia was not in the best interest of the government. However, the main reasons must have been economic. Lucrative markets were in Austrian lands and beyond, not in Serbia.

As European industry developed, raw materials naturally went from the less advanced economy, Bosnia, to the more advanced economy, Austria. Physical proximity made economic exchange between Bosnia and the Austrian domains inevitable, aided considerably by the difficulty of transporting goods to the rest of the Ottoman empire. Cargoes traveled to Austrian ports on the Adriatic coast or north to Croatia. During the latter half of the century the northern sanjak of Banaluka in particular became integrated into the Austrian economy. In 1872 a railroad was constructed from Banaluka to Novi, on the Austrian border. From the 1860s on, Ottoman governors built improved roads that connected interior cities with routes to the north, not notably to the south.

The most obvious candidate for export from Bosnia was lumber, but merchants could not transport lumber in bulk until roads had been improved. Thus, even through Herzegovina had abundant forests, throughout the Ottoman period its exports were primarily animal products—hides, fur, sheep—and some tobacco and other crops, not wood. In the north, on the other hand, Banaluka began to prosper because of improved transportation. European ships on the Sava River brought goods, which were transshipped by land to Banaluka. Lumber became the principal export north. Small private industries—especially those based on wood, such as sawmills and woodworking—sprang up. As elsewhere, most of the new commerce was in the hands of Christian merchants, who were the preferred partners of the European Christians. All was tied into the Austrian economy.

HISTORY

An Ottoman official looking at a map of Bosnia in 1800 might have despaired. Bosnia was in such a dismal geographic position that any Ottoman leader would have thought twice before committing resources to it that could be spent on more secure places. Geographically, it was far removed from the center of Ottoman authority. Sarajevo was almost twice as far from Istanbul as it was from Vienna, the Austro-Hungarian capital; Belgrade, the Serbian capital, was four times closer than Istanbul; Bosnia's northern districts were closer to Berlin than they were to Istanbul. This might have had little effect on Ottoman rule of the province if the Ottoman empire had had adequate military power and modern transportation, but it had neither. The Austrian empire, on the other hand, surrounded Bosnia on two sides. If Austria claimed Bosnia, the Ottomans could not save it.

Like Albania and Montenegro, Bosnia was an inherently difficult region to rule. Its mountainous terrain made it possible for small groups to resist large armies. The Ottomans had early developed a policy of rule that allowed Bosnian leaders a great degree of autonomy. As long as a satisfactory sum was sent to the central treasury each year, it was less expensive for the government to accept the status quo than to mount a major pacification campaign. This became more and more true as the Ottoman central authority declined in the seventeenth and eighteenth centuries.

By 1800, political authority in Bosnia had for some time been held by hereditary Muslim notables, called *kapudan*s (captains). The *kapudan* system had evolved from the Ottoman *tîmâr* system that involved giving military leaders control of conquered lands and allowing them to use the proceeds from the lands to support their soldiers. The soldiers were to keep the peace in the region and make themselves available when the sultan called them to war. Because they were on the military marches with Austria, the *kapudan*s were organized into local military units whose main purpose was the defense of Bosnia. They became an integrated part of the Bosnian political and military system.

When the Ottoman central government was strong, abuses

of the *kapudan* system were kept in check. The *kapudans* and other Muslim notables were subject to Ottoman laws designed to secure central government control and to ensure just treatment of peasants so that they would stay on the land to support the economy and maintain the tax base. In the eighteenth century, however, the *kapudans* and lesser notables largely succeeded in keeping their control over their lands while ignoring the legal rights both of the peasants and of the sultan. Because the sultan's government was too weak to assert its prerogatives, Bosnian notables were able illegally to convert crown lands into private holdings. Acting as a corporation,[7] the *kapudans* ruled Bosnia for their personal benefit.

Both the central government and the peasantry suffered. Abuses were ubiquitous. Laws that limited the amount of taxes that could be collected from peasants or the amount of corvée labor demanded of them did not function in the absence of central authority. Bosnia remained a part of the Ottoman empire, but in reality Ottoman law no longer applied.

In many ways the Bosnians remained loyal subjects of the sultan. They never relinquished their duties as defenders of the Ottoman borders, and they continued to provide soldiers for the sultan's wars. Ironically, this made it all the more difficult for the central government to assert its control over the province, because the Ottomans depended on the military contribution of the autonomous Bosnians. As the strength of the Janissaries and other military units declined in the seventeenth and eighteenth centuries, the government counted more and more on local forces of Albanians, Bosnians, and Crimean Tatars to fight its wars: it was Bosnians and Albanians, for example, who went to Egypt with Muhammad Ali to fight the French invaders. An Ottoman expedition to bring Bosnia back to central control would not only have been horrendously expensive, it would also have cost the empire some of its best troops. Better, from the Ottoman perspective, to leave them alone, and in essence the Ottomans did leave Bosnia alone until the nineteenth century.

Bosnia, Serbia, and Montenegro

Bosnia's history is intimately involved with that of Serbia and Montenegro. Beginning in the eighteenth century, the Serbs of Montenegro and Serbia rebelled repeatedly to gain first autonomy within the Ottoman empire and then independence. As those two Ottoman provinces rebelled, they drew Bosnia into their conflicts with the central government. Serbs claimed Bosnia because it had been part of ancient Serbian kingdoms and because they saw it as an essential link in the geography of a greater Serbia, tying together Serbia and Montenegro and perhaps even extending to ports on the Adriatic. The large minority of Serbs in Bosnia were viewed as "unredeemed"—Serbs who still had to be drawn into the national fold.

Together with the Bosnian notables, ethnic Serbian rebels were the other force that stood in the way of Ottoman rule in Bosnia. Montenegran raids into Bosnia and Bosnian raids into Montenegro were so common in the first half of the nineteenth century they amounted to a continuous war. As it strove for its own independence, Serbia sent agitators into Bosnia to encourage Serbs there to join in the fight. Intercommunal warfare sometimes resulted. When Serbs rebelled in the early nineteenth century, for example, they attacked Muslim villages. The Bosnian Muslims then joined Sultan Mahmud II's army in putting down the Serbian revolt. In the Serbian revolts that extended into the 1820s the 15,000 to 20,000 Muslims resident in Serbia fled or were expelled, replaced by Serbs from Bosnia. When the European powers forced the Ottomans to accept Serbian autonomy in 1833 Bosnian lands were given to Serbia.

The greatest danger posed by Serbian unrest was the threat of European intervention that always accompanied it. Throughout the nineteenth century, rebellions by Christians were the first step in the loss of Ottoman provinces, always through European intervention. While the Ottomans could and did hold off both Serbia and Montenegro militarily, experience had taught them that the European powers might take Bosnia away from the Ottomans, no matter what the outcome on the battlefield. Austria always presented the greatest danger. It was a European power with greater economic ties to Bosnia than the Ottomans had. Moreover, Austria had no desire to see Serbia seize Bosnia and to avoid it might make a preemptive strike. Only the European balance of power kept the Austrians from taking the province. Should that balance of power change, Ottoman Bosnia was at risk. Ultimately, however, it was rebellion of Serbs in Bosnia and war with Serbia that led the Ottomans to lose Bosnia.

Ottoman Reform and Reassertion of Ottoman Power in Bosnia

When the Ottoman empire set firmly on a course of reform in the reign of Sultan Mahmud II (1808–39), Bosnian notables wanted no part of it. The primary purpose of the reforms was to increase the power of the central government and to turn the Ottoman state into a centralized state similar to those in Europe. It was in their interest to oppose that since ultimately there was no place in a reform empire for independent lords who withheld tax monies and did not wish their men to be drafted into the imperial forces. Reform meant the end of their power and independence, and the notables realized this. During his reign, Mahmud II had destroyed the power of independent notables in Bulgaria, southern Albania, and Anatolia whose positions had been analogous to that of the Bosnian lords.

There were also emotional reasons for the Bosnians to reject reform. The Muslims of Bosnia were religiously conservative.

Since the exile of Muslims after the Austrian conquests at the end of the seventeenth century, the European Christians had been the enemy. Like others in such a position, they held fast to their own religious traditions. The reforms proclaimed in Istanbul were by nature "infidel" reforms because their intent was to copy European ways to strengthen the empire. This was seen as a threat to Islam.

The first attempts at reform in Bosnia came in 1826. In that year Mahmud II disbanded the Janissaries in Istanbul and throughout the empire. But in Bosnia the notables protected the Janissaries from the sultan and refused to cooperate with reform. When the sultan attempted to conscript Bosnians for his new European-style army, the Bosnian notables revolted. The sultan first tried to conciliate the notables but was then forced to send an army to the province. The notables were crushed in 1831. The victory allowed Mahmud to extend imperial control and to abolish the *kapudan* system in 1835; the Bosnian soldiers were gradually integrated into the Ottoman army. The taxes once collected by the notables were now collected by the government.

Angered by their continued loss of power, the Bosnian notables revolted in 1849 and again in 1850, bringing another intervention by the Ottoman military. The system of Europeanizing reforms known as the Tanzimat had begun in Istanbul. The Ottoman forces that put down the rebels came to Bosnia with imperial orders to apply the new reforms, which regularized the judiciary under the central authority of Istanbul and organized the administrative districts. Authority was put into the hands of administrators from the Ottoman civil service, not, as in the past, local Bosnian notables. The bureaucrats would run each sanjak and answer to Istanbul. As was the case all over the empire during the Tanzimat period, a written set of administrative regulations took the place of ad hoc rules. The new rules included the appointment of an administrative council on which sat both Muslims and Christians who would advise the governor, and bureaucrats had to go by the book.

After a rebellion by Christian peasants in 1858, the Porte put into place further, primarily centralizing, reforms. In particular, new Ottoman laws on land tenure and provincial organization that had heretofore not been applied in Bosnia were now put into place. Another revolt, in Herzegovina, which had festered since 1852, was put down in 1861. In 1862, the privileges of Bosnian Christians were extended to match those long enjoyed by non-Muslims in the rest of the empire, including the right openly to operate Christian schools and to open new churches. These reforms alleviated somewhat the hard life of the Christian peasantry. Some Tanzimat economic reforms were put in place, including government-run "banks" that made loans to villagers. The situation in Bosnia was slowly brought into line with that of the rest of the empire.

Contributing to Ottoman difficulties in reforming Bosnia was continuing civil unrest. Montenegran revolts against the Ottomans disrupted life and government in Bosnia as well as Montenegro. Montenegran troops invaded Herzegovina in 1860, slaughtering Muslim villagers until they were defeated by the Ottomans. Unrest, especially among Bosnian Serbs, persisted throughout the 1860s and 1870s. Notwithstanding the disruption from Montenegran and Serbian actions, the revolts were ultimately beneficial to Ottoman control. In Bosnia, where both notables and ordinary Muslims were hostile to Ottoman reform, a significant military force was needed to implement them. The soldiers were sent to defeat the revolt of the notables, then to defeat Montenegro, but they also provided the military backbone for reform. Ömer Pasha and Osman Pasha, in particular, made use of the force at their command to bring about change.

Ottoman reform took firm hold in the 1860s. During the short governorship of Ömer Lütfi Pasha (1860–61), the last vestiges of the military power of the landlords finally disappeared, allowing the introduction of the Tanzimat reforms. Topal Osman Pasha, who followed Ömer Pasha as governor from 1861–69, was able to reorganize the administration of the province and generally improve central government control. The provincial capital was shifted from Travnik—considered to be the center of the traditionalist opposition to reform—to Sarajevo.

The governorships of the pashas Ömer and Osman marked the end of the traditionalists' active opposition to the authority of the central government and to reform. This did not mean that great changes were immediately introduced. It proved impossible, for example, for the Ottomans completely to end the traditional system of land tenure—a system that robbed both the peasants of Bosnia and the central government. Tentative attempts to introduce reform in the landlord-tenant relationship were insignificant, and the attempt to abolish tax-farming was a complete failure, as it proved immensely difficult to alter a centuries-old system. Tax farms could not be abolished until detailed registers of cultivators had been drawn up and basic decisions made as to who would own the land. The traditional system was too engrained to be reformed quickly. Government undertakings to improve manufacturing in Bosnia also had little success. Rug factories and the like that the government sponsored were actually little more than substitutes for traditional crafts. Merchants were aided by government loans, but in general manufacturing in Bosnia fell afoul of the same problems that afflicted business throughout the Ottoman empire: local goods could not compete with less expensive merchandise made in Europe, and taxation was weighted against local businessmen. Because of the Capitulations and internal duties on goods passing between provinces, European merchants bringing in goods from abroad paid lower customs duty than Ottoman merchants bringing goods from another Ottoman province. The combination of a low level of technology and education and high internal taxation made industrialization all but impossible. Despite failures, however, the Ottomans did effect real reform, and some of the reforms significantly improved the province's economic life. In 1860, Sarajevo was connected to the Ottoman and European telegraph systems. The city's first printing press was put in operation in 1865. The road system was improved in much of the province. These were the first steps toward bringing Bosnia into the modern transportation and communication systems of Europe. Trade, particularly trade with Austria, increased markedly. While the old system of land tenure remained, it was regularized throughout the province in 1848 and further codified in 1859, to the benefit of both peasants and the government. Peasants on crown lands were guaranteed the right to leave the land, and landlords were given greater security of tenure (these reforms did not affect privately owned land). Administratively, the entire operation of the province was revolutionized. The Ottoman provincial law of 1864 was put into place in Bosnia, ordering the province into small, governable units with a regulated chain of authority among officials. Advisory councils of local leaders of the various religious communities were established. In short, reform was proceeding, if slowly, when the Austrians took the province in 1878. Bosnia in 1878 was very different from Bosnia in 1880.

The End of Ottoman Bosnia

The 1875 Serbian rebellion in Bosnia spelled the end to Ottoman rule. The rebellion began as a protest against landlords in Herzegovina and soon spread to the rest of Bosnia province. The first actions of the Serbian rebels were against tax collectors, landlords, and Ottoman officials, and they found sympathy even among Muslim peasants. However, the character of the rebellion soon changed with attacks on Muslim villages and counter-attacks on Serbs. The rebellion turned into a large-scale guerilla and intercommunal war between Muslims and Serbs. The rebels were at first supported by Montenegro and by pan-Slavist elements in Russia. Guns came from Montenegro and through Austria-Hungary. The Ottoman response to the rebellion was tempered by this European intervention. In December 1875, Austria, Germany, and Russia ("the League of the Three Emperors") demanded that the Ottomans conciliate the rebels by abolishing tax farming, lowering taxes, and making other reforms. The Ottomans agreed to the demands and issued a pardon for the rebels. This had little effect. The rebellion continued. At that point the Ottoman government sent Ahmet Muhtar Pasha with an army and put down the rebellion by force. Distressed by accounts of Christian refugees fleeing to surrounding countries (and ignoring, as they had throughout the rebellion, any Muslim suffering), the European powers made a new set of demands on the Ottomans in May of 1876. Meanwhile, events in Bulgaria had altered the situation.

The Bulgarian revolution of 1876 and the subsequent Russo-Turkish War of 1877–78 decided the fate of Ottoman Bosnia. The Ottoman suppression of Bulgarians, who rebelled in May 1876, inflamed European public opinion against the Ottomans. Prince Milan of Serbia, influenced both by Russia and by popular anti-Turkish sentiment in Serbia, allied with Montenegro and attacked the Ottoman empire. In August of 1876 the Ottomans defeated the Serbs. The Ottomans had thus been successful in defeating rebellions in both Bosnia and Bulgaria and in defeating Serbia and Montenegro. Russia was unwilling to accept such a setback to its plans for independent Slavic states in the Balkans. After diplomatic efforts to avoid war failed, Russia declared war on the Ottoman empire on 24 April 1877.

Bosnia was a bargaining chip in the war. In order to ensure Austria-Hungary's neutrality in the war, the Russians agreed that the Austrians could occupy Bosnia-Herzegovina. The Ottomans were defeated in 1878 and forced to sign the Treaty of San Stephano, but because Austria and other European powers decided that the terms of the treaty were against their interests, they forced Russia to accept new terms at the Congress of Berlin (13 June–13 July 1878). The congress awarded Bosnia and Herzegovina to Austria, less a part of Herzegovina, which went to Montenegro. In theory, Austria was only to occupy the province, which would still remain technically under Ottoman sovereignty. In fact, Bosnia became an Austrian colony. On 21 April 1879, Sultan Abdülhamid II formally accepted the status of Bosnia as an Austrian protectorate. Bosnian Muslim uprisings against the Austrian occupation were unsuccessful.

The inhabitants of Bosnia paid a heavy price for the events of 1875 to 1878. The death rate among the Serbs and especially the Muslims was very high. That, combined with emigration, changed the ethnic makeup of Bosnia forever.

Comparisons between the populations of Ottoman and Austrian-controlled Bosnia cannot be exact because the provincial boundaries were not the same. Austrian Bosnia was smaller than Ottoman Bosnia. Parts of the Hersek sanjak had been awarded to Montenegro in 1878, and the Yenipazar sanjak remained in the Ottoman empire. Nevertheless, a close approximation is possible. Subtracting a quarter of the Hersek Muslim population and all of the Yenipazar Muslim population from the Muslim population figures in table 3.2 leaves a Muslim population of the area of Austrian-controlled Bosnia of approximately 695,000 in 1870 (see table 3.4). The Austrian census of 1879 recorded only 449,000 Muslims in Bosnia. A great number of the Muslims had gone.

As table 3.4 indicates, Bosnia must have suffered greatly in the rebellion that began in 1875. The Serbian population declined appreciably (7 percent is the estimate in table 3.4). The Muslim population suffered a far worse decline, a loss of more

Table 3.4   The Population of Bosnia* in 1870 and 1879

	1870	1879
Muslim	694,000	449,000
Orthodox	534,000	496,485
Catholic	208,000	209,000

Source: Table 3.2 and Austrian Census of 1895.
*The area of Bosnia controlled by Austria after 1878.

than one third. Many Muslims migrated to the Ottoman empire after the Austrian occupation, and many must have died in the 1875 revolt. The figures for 1870, which are approximations, may be somewhat high or the Austrian enumeration somewhat low but in either case have small effect on the magnitude of the population loss.

The Bosnia captured by the Austrians was significantly different than Ottoman Bosnia in 1800. Ottoman reform efforts had changed civil authority in the province, removing power from the hands of local notables, although the government had not been able to remove economic power from the traditional landlords. A slight start had been made in bringing modern education to the province. Transportation by road was improved, and a start had even been made on railroad transport. Bosnia in 1878 was more integrated into the European economic system than would have been conceivable in 1800. Despite changes and reforms, however, Bosnia still remained one of the least developed Ottoman provinces. In Ottoman Europe, only Albania could compare in lack of development.

The most significant difference in Bosnia before and after the troubles of 1875–78 was demographic. In 1870 the Muslims of Ottoman Bosnia had been the largest group in the population, making up only slightly less than 50 percent of the total. In

1879 the Orthodox Serbs were the largest religious group: the province that had been almost 50 percent Muslim in 1870 was now more than 60 percent Christian. This constituted the most significant change in Bosnia since the Ottoman conquest four hundred years earlier.

NOTES

1. The name Bosnia is used here to signify the Ottoman Bosna vilayet, which included Herzegovina and the sanjak of Yenipazar (Novipazar) in addition to Bosnia proper.
2. Yenipazar was originally divided between Serbia and Montenegro in the treaty of San Stephano, but the Congress of Berlin overthrew the award.
3. The process of correction normally used for an Ottoman population depends on the availability of data by age group and over a number of years. Because neither of these are available for Bosnia, I have assumed that the Bosnian population was undercounted as much as was the case in the closest Ottoman province, Kosova (see McCarthy, 1990). Note that the seemingly precise numbers in the table are a product of the correction process, not an indication of precision to the last person.
4. The material on housing here has been drawn from those sources and from various works on Ottoman housing, particularly the writings of Vedat Eldem.
5. Most authors call the Bosnian sharecropper system serfdom and the relationship between peasant and landlord feudal. However, few of the circumstances and laws that characterized European feudalism applied in the Ottoman Empire.
6. Hersek sanjak is not included in these figures.
7. Some sources claim there were 39 *kapudan* families, others say 36.

REFERENCES

Arbuthnot, Lieut. G. (1862). *Herzegovina: or Omer Pacha and the Christian Rebels*. London.

Birken, Andreas. (1976). *Die Provinzen des Osmanischen Reiches.* Wiesbaden.

Cvijić, Jovan. (1918). *La Péninsule balkanique: géographie humaine.* Paris.

Danes, Georg V. (1903). *Bevölkerungsdichtigkeit der Hercegovina.* Prague.

McCarthy, Justin. (1990). "The Population of Ottoman Europe Before and After the Fall of the Empire." In Heath W. Lowry and Ralph S. Hattox, *Third Congress on the Social and Economic History of Turkey.* Istanbul.

Thurnher, Majda. (1956). "A Survey of Balkan Houses and Farm Buildings." *Kroeber Anthropological Society Papers,* 14 (Spring), 19–92.

FOUR

The Muslims of Bosnia-Herzegovina Under Austro-Hungarian Rule, 1878–1918

Mark Pinson

Harvard University

The previous chapters in this book have dealt with the emergence and development of the Bosnian Muslim community under the rule of a coreligionist government. In the Austrian period, Bosnian Islam for the first time had to deal with non-Muslim rulers, a condition that persisted from 1878 to the collapse of Yugoslavia in 1992. Since I will present only some aspects of the history of Bosnia-Herzegovina and of its Muslim population in the Austrian period rather than a straightforward chronological history, a few methodological explanations are in order here.

The foci of this chapter will be (1) significant developments in the history of the three main players—the Bosnian Muslims, Austria, and the Ottoman Empire just before 1878; (2) Austrian policy in the new province; (3) development of the Bosnian Muslim identity in traditional and new forms; (4) administration and economic development of Bosnia; and (5) complexities in the relationship with the Turkish state.

Comparative analysis has a role to play in understanding

developments in this area.[1] Since other chapters provide the possibility of "vertical" comparisons in time, in this chapter, for this period, I have tried to provide the basis for "horizontal" comparisons of Austrian successes and failures with those of its ally and rival, Russia, with similar problems in nearby regions, in this period or shortly before it. Since Bosnia for almost all of its history has been under the rule of some other state, this kind of historical analysis may be of interest to readers curious about the extent of possible successful intervention by an outside power in this region, even when that power has the tactical advantage of being an absolutist empire rather than a democracy. This is admittedly history writing under the sign of present developments rather than more conventional academic history; however, this volume is intended to reach a wider public as well as fellow historians.[2]

Since this text is to be for a general readership, the usual laborious academic apparatus of extensive footnoting has been dispensed with. At the end of this chapter is a brief list of English-language works that cover aspects of Bosnia addressed in this study.

When I began to review works on this subject, I was under the impression that any number of historical works in English on Yugoslavia to which readers could be referred for a background overview of this period. On closer examination, it emerged that many works had chapters on Bosnia in this period but that coverage was overwhelmingly, where not exclusively, on the diplomatic maneuverings of the great powers and some of the Balkan states—with little or no attention given to internal developments in Bosnia. To help remedy this situation for both general readers and specialists in Islamic studies, most of whom do not read Serbian, I am exploring the possibility of having translated from Serbian into English several articles and books by local Bosnian historians on the Muslim community in the Ottoman, Austrian, and Yugoslav periods.

Finally, throughout the text *Bosnia* and *Bosnian* will be used to stand for Bosnia-Herzegovina and *Austria* for the Austro-Hungarian empire. Where the focus is narrower, the text will make this clear.

THE BACKGROUND: THE AUSTRIAN AND OTTOMAN EMPIRES AND THE BOSNIAN MUSLIMS

Certain developments in Habsburg domestic and foreign policy did much to produce the annexation and influence the character of the occupation. In the 1860s in the Habsburg empire, two non-German nationalities underwent superficially similar changes in status not shared by any other non-German nationalities. The *Ausgleich*, or compromise, of 1867 made Hungary an equal partner with the Austrians in the newly defined dual monarchy. In 1868 a small-scale rerun, called the *Nagodba* (also compromise) between Hungary and its subject nationality, the Croats, was proclaimed, but this compromise in no way gave the Croats equal status with the Hungarians in the kingdom of Hungary comparable to what the *Ausgleich* gave the Hungarians in the whole empire. Although these changes gave two nationalities a new kind of recognition, albeit to varying degrees, they did not represent a trend away from monarchic rule toward something resembling participatory democracy or anything of the sort. If anything, in the decades just before 1878, the direction of internal policy had been toward a kind of bureaucratic authoritarianism.

In foreign policy, Austria in midcentury had two significant concerns vis-à-vis the Balkans: (1) to keep Russian presence and influence to a minimum and (2) to maintain the status quo with the Ottoman administration. In the years that followed, however, the likelihood that the Ottomans could hold out against Serbia, with or without foreign aid, appeared to decline, and the emergence of a powerful unified Germany in 1871 ended any Austrian expansion that had been possible in the earlier miasma of small German states. The only direction for Austrian expansion lay, then, to the south into Bosnia; it was made all the more appealing by the possibility that if Austria did not seize the opportunity, Serbia and Montenegro might take over Bosnia and form a significant basis for a large South Slav state, which in turn could become a magnet for the Slavic populations in the adjacent Austro-Hungarian provinces.

Gyula Andrassy, the imperial foreign minister in the 1870s, and his colleague, Benjamin Kallay, later prominent as head of the Austrian administration in Bosnia, were both Hungarians. The Hungarians in their half of the empire were substantially outnumbered by non-Hungarians there, mostly Slavs of various sorts and Romanians. With this feeling of already nearly drowning in a non-Hungarian sea, one of the last things these Hungarians wanted was to bring more Slavs into the empire, and there were also Austrians who thought this way. But in the summer of 1878, Andrassy faced a situation in which Russia, by creating the large, but short-lived so-called San Stefano Bulgaria, had violated an earlier agreement not to foster the creation of a large Balkan state. The only way Andrassy saw to redress the balance was to implement another part of that same agreement that provided for the Austrian annexation of Bosnia at any time convenient for Austria. It was the desire to block the formation of a large South Slav state, then, that probably did much to move Austria to carry out this occupation, which under other circumstances it might not have done.

The Ottoman empire was the state from whose actual control Bosnia-Herzegovina had just been taken and under whose nominal suzerainty it continued, at least in theory, to remain until 1908. The Ottomans were now in a new and difficult position with regard to the Bosnian Muslims. While European states had had long experience in intervening, not always from a position of strength, with Muslim rulers on behalf of local Christians, the first Ottoman intervention with a Christian state on behalf of Muslims had come only a few decades earlier involving Muslims in several areas around the Black Sea under Russian control or in process of being conquered. Two other factors, besides relative inexperience, were to make successful intervention hard for the Ottomans: (1) only a few decades earlier the Ottomans had created Western-style ministries, such as Foreign Affairs, and resident embassies abroad; and (2) although the myth of the continually victorious Ottoman state, prevalent in earlier centuries, had taken quite a pounding since the late seventeenth century, one suspects that at times during the nineteenth century some remnants of the old myth interfered with sober political judgment. So by the late nineteenth century, although the Russians had had a great deal of experience creating a basis for intervention on behalf of coreligionists and then expanding it in various diplomatic ways over many years, the Ottomans were new at the game. Not surprisingly they had little real impact on developments, remaining mainly an unplayed card of indefinite potential in the minds of some Bosnian Muslims.

The Ottoman-Bosnian relationship had another aspect that was to make the new, isolated, and exposed position of the Bosnian Muslims difficult. The Ottoman empire had been an essentially non-national state; its subjects were grouped by religion, not nationality. In the century before 1878, those territories of the Ottoman empire that were in Europe had seen the emergence of nationalism; it had become, in the minds of some of the subject populations, in some contexts more important than religion. The Balkan Orthodox groups in the nineteenth century came at times to show much more concern for their future as a national group than the cohesion of the Orthodox population in the empire as a whole. The clearest illustrations of this were the conflicts of varying intensity between the newly emerged "national" churches and the patriarchate in Istanbul.

Elsewhere in the empire, even in the dominant Muslim millet—e.g., in parts of the Arab world—for some early nationalists
"Muslim millet-hood" was becoming an insufficient identity.
The exception of this trend was the Muslim community of
Bosnia-Herzegovina, which in 1878 ceased essentially to be
under Muslim rule and, although Slav in several significant
respects, was not in the main interested in becoming part of
any of the new Slavic states. For them the main differentiating
factor was religion, Islam, rather than ethnicity, Slavic. When
the area was no longer under a Muslim suzerain, this created
for the powers that tried to deal with Bosnia-Herzegovina a
problem quite different from other problems in this area. The
substitution among Bosnian Muslims of religion for national
identity, in contrast to the Christian Serbs and Croats in Bosnia-
Herzegovina, is an added complication on which a few observers, then and now, have remarked, but to which many others
appear to have been oblivious. One important aspect of the
relatively short Austro-Hungarian period for the historical development of the Bosnian Muslim collective identity is that since
this was the first period of non-Ottoman rule, it was the one in
which the need to define themselves in this way and the attendant problems of self-definition emerged. Because Bosnia's Muslim leaders had been linked to the religious authorities in Istanbul, they also did not have the kind of fully articulated local
organization in place that the Orthodox and the Catholics had
at the beginning of the occupation; this proved to be another
handicap for the Muslims.

Robert Donia, one of the major students of the history of the
Bosnian Muslims in this period, notes that the political awakening of the Bosnian Muslims was unlike the Eastern European
nationalist revivals. It was not preceded by large-scale social
changes, such as increased urbanization, industrialization, and
literacy, or the emergence of either a formal ideology or dominant spokesman. The very word *revival* suggests another difference. The Greeks, Croats, Czechs, and Bulgarians, all had a

historical state in the past to harken back to. Even though none of those medieval states had been remotely populist democracies in which the *vox populi* was *vox Dei*—in most cases they were absolute monarchies—they did have certain features in common. The dominant group could look back to a golden age in history and had a national language, so that politicians, publicists, and others could find a basis for the creation of a national culture, literature, and church.

The Bosnian Muslims had no such institution or period in their collective memory. Medieval Bosnia, while including some of their ethnic ancestors, had been Christian and so to some extent invalid as a national image. Earlier Muslim states, acceptable from the religious point of view, had been the creations of Arabs or Turks and could not be the objects of total identification for Bosnian Slavic Muslims. The early heroic epics of other Muslims could have been little known among Bosnian Muslims and could not serve the functions that national epics did for other groups. Modern perspectives may distort one's understanding of this latter point. Not only were their creations not of "one's own," but literacy in Serbian was limited and in Ottoman Turkish much more so. For those who could read, printing in Serbian and Ottoman were still in the early stages; other modern conveniences such as imports or translations of major works were nonexistent. The first printing shop in Bosnia was set up by a printer from the Vojvodina only in 1866; it produced mainly school books and materials for the government. Two newspapers appeared in Serbian, but even by the mid-1870s Sarajevo, with a population of some 50,000, had no bookshops.[3] *Political awakening* is a more appropriate term for what was going on in Bosnia since it does not include elements subsumed under the term *national revival* so central to other Eastern European groups. Another important element differentiating this movement from national revivals in Eastern Europe is that, in the absence of some remote medieval state,

Bosnian Muslims had no "Greater X" myth (e.g., *Megale Idea, Velika B'lgariia,* or *Büyük Türkiye*) suggesting or dictating borders, which in other cases in Eastern Europe were often as generous as they were vague. This absence of an earlier prototypical state with borders that had enjoyed at least some kind of recognition might have contributed in later periods to anxiety over recognition of boundaries and border areas.

Many national groups of Eastern Europe had survived long periods of foreign rule, after which they had emerged to begin a new national political and cultural existence. They could, with varying degrees of success, survive foreign rule, whether of other national Christian groups or of the Ottomans who differed both in nationality and religion. Bosnian Muslims not only lacked any such reassuring historical lessons to look back on, but they also were, to some extent, divided on the basic question of whether Islam allowed them to live under Christian rule at all. In the absence of anything even remotely resembling public opinion surveys, one cannot say with any certainty how many persons were influenced by such thoughts, although figures on emigration may indicate some degree of concern. It is, however, certain that Bosnian Muslim society faced this particular problem for the first time at the beginning of this period and that, however many of these Muslims gave any thought to it, it may well have been a factor making for more intense and less conciliatory national positions.

AUSTRIAN POLICIES:
LOCAL INFLUENCES AND CONSTRAINTS

In another regard, it was Austria that was new at the game— as the last European state to assume control of an area with a significant Muslim population. Britain, France, Holland, and Russia already had done so in the Near East, Far East, Central

Asia, and North Africa. In most of those cases the Europeans had simply conquered the area; in the Austrian case, control was formally at least somewhat limited, until the outright annexation thirty years later. One reflection of this somewhat anomalous status was visible at the highest level of governance of the new province. When the question arose whether to integrate the new territory into the Austrian half or the Hungarian half a strange compromise was reached: the territory ended up under the control of the Joint Imperial Finance Ministry—that is, not under either Austria or Hungary, like almost all of the rest of the empire, but under an imperial institution. One consequence of this was that the province was subject to the assemblies of both halves of the empire, which slowed implementation of policy. Another reflection of this status was that the supreme on-site authority for most of the period, per a decree of September 1882, was the commander-in-chief of the Fifteenth Army Corps in Sarajevo. Under him was the civil *adlatus* (aide-de-camp), who controlled the civil administration.

Another reflection of the unusual nature of the governance was an approach to the previous local administration that we might call "institutional tinkering" rather than a full-fledged all-out effort to bring everything into line with standard *k.u.k.* practice immediately. There was, when dealing with matters Muslim, a tendency to begin reform by trying only to regularize, in the Austrian view, extant Muslim institutions and practices as they were, to leave them in place but bring their level of administrative practice up to those of other parts of the Austro-Hungarian bureaucracy.

Another factor influencing the Austrian administration in several ways was the structure of the population. Peter Sugar (1963), a leading student of the economic history of Bosnia-Herzegovina in this period, observed that the Ottoman census figure of 1,051,000 for Bosnia in 1875 seemed low. The second Austrian census ten years later yielded 1,336,091, and the decade in between had been one of revolt and war, in which Bosnia and Herzegovina were not islands of tranquility to which the war weary would flee, but theaters of conflict from which people would depart. Sugar mentioned as one indication of this a report by the French consul in 1880 that of the 200,000 estimated to have fled Bosnia-Herzegovina during the war, some 130,000 had not yet returned. If one were to accept the Ottoman figure, then the postwar number of Bosnians would have been about 1,466,000 (the 1885 population plus 130,000 refugees elsewhere). This would mean that the increase in population between 1875 (1,051,000) and 1885 (1,466,000) would have been somewhat over 400,000 or more than a third in ten years, a rate that would have been exceptional in a war-torn area. Even the hastiest calculation will suffice to show that there are problems with both sets of figures. They are mentioned here just to give a general idea of the size of the population and to highlight something of the nature of the statistics from the region.

According to the 1879 census, the Muslims were included in the Slavic group, and further attempts to subdivide them on the basis of available data were not successful. The religious groups were Muslims, 38 percent, Orthodox, 42 percent, Roman Catholic, 18 percent, and Jewish, 0.25 percent. While the specific numbers changed over time, certain aspects remained constant: no group had a majority, the Orthodox and Muslim groups were far and away the largest and more or less the same proportion of the total.

One remarkable aspect of the advent of Austrian rule was that suddenly the smallest of the three—the Roman Catholics—became the coreligionists of the ruling power, and the Muslims, who formerly held that distinction, now found themselves both demoted and in an ambiguous situation. Although in practical terms Ottoman control had ended, until the formal annexation of Bosnia-Herzegovina by the Austrians, the Ottomans retained nominal suzerainty. This meant that for the first thirty years of Austrian rule, the Muslims did not feel totally isolated or subordinated, since at least in theory they could have recourse to their ultimate suzerain, the Ottoman empire, should they be displeased by measures taken by the occupying Austrians.

The first Austrian census did not break the population down by profession, but the second one did; according to it 2.06 percent of the population were landlords, 29.75 percent were free peasants, 50 percent were *kmet*s (that is, peasants who were bound to the land, and liable for a broad range of taxes and service obligations to the local landlord), and 18 percent had some other occupation. From this it is clear that the vast majority, some 80 percent, were involved in agriculture.

The last significant group, though not in numerical terms, of Bosnian Muslims were the emigrés. Bosnian emigration to Turkey appears to have gone on rather steadily with peaks in years of exceptional stress, that is, immediately after the occupation of 1878; after the announcement of general conscription in 1881–82 (when an estimated 8,000 emigrated), in 1900–1, after the political upheavals (when some 13,000 left), and after formal annexation in 1908 (when some 28,000 departed). According to one Bosnian historian, in all about 140,000 emigrated to Turkey between 1878 and 1918. Since those who most actively resisted Austrian rule came from groups already small in number—large landholders, clerics, townspeople, and emigrés—this was no mass movement. Many of them were in Anatolia, far from the action in Istanbul.

The structure of the local population put the Austrians, after 1878, in an unprecedented situation in the Balkans. In the seventeenth and eighteenth centuries, when Austria conquered Hungary and northern parts of what was later Yugoslavia, which had earlier been occupied by the Ottomans, there was no large Muslim population interested in maintaining either essentially Ottoman institutions, such as those of local government, or purely Islamic institutions, such as mosques, Muslim clergy, or sharia courts, which had been maintained by the Ottoman government. This was not the case in Bosnia, where a significant portion of the wealth of local elites was based on lands they held under Ottoman rule or paid administrative posts managing vakifs they had held and where the general Muslim population wanted to preserve all Muslim institutions. This was a significant factor in the Austrian decision to proceed cautiously, steering a slow course among three options: (1) leaving these institutions in place, even though they corresponded little to Austrian practice, and so providing minimal provocation for local Muslims; (2) eliminating them quickly and totally and replacing them as completely as possible with standard Austrian institutions, a procedure that would have been bound to produce maximum antipathy and possibly even resistance; or (3) leaving them in place and trying gradually to phase out some and modify others to bring them into conformity with standard Habsburg administrative practice. For example, the vakifs were allowed to continue to function, though the Austrian administration tried to introduce somewhat more precise bookkeeping methods than had previously been the case.

One noteworthy example of such a compromise or innovation that was part of the Austrian effort to wean the Muslims away from the religious establishment in Istanbul was the creation of a local supreme religious authority, the *reis ul-ulema,* and a four-man council, the *mejlis al-ulema.* But the fig leaf was only partially successful: many Muslims did not consider them authentic spiritual leaders because they had been appointed by the Austrians, not the Ottomans.

The Austrian administration mainly chose the third alternative. While it might well have reduced initial resistance to Austrian rule, it also meant that debate and conflict over the nature and fate of Ottoman or Muslim institutions was to go on for many years. One consequence of this was that for some thirty years Muslim-Habsburg conflict functioned as a kind of incubator for Bosnian Muslim national identity both in the discussions among the Muslims and their struggles over the role and scope of the old Muslim institutions or new ones that appeared in this period, such as political parties.

ASSERTION OF BOSNIAN MUSLIM IDENTITY

One of the most striking changes among the Muslims came in the forms of power in the Bosnian Muslim society—namely, the emergence of the political party. Donia (1981), whose work traced this process in detail, began his discussion of this by presenting the concept of personal networks, developed by some social scientists as essential to his discussion, explaining that the Bosnian elites, in the Ottoman period, functioned at home and in Istanbul largely through such personal networks, what we might call connections. He mentioned that some students of structural social development have advanced the idea that one important difference between older societies and the more modern Western ones is the greater number and scope of institutions in the latter to carry out various functions and the resulting greater reliance by citizens of states on such institutions, rather than on personal connections, to achieve their goals, as in traditional societies. Viewed in this perspective, the creation by the Muslims in this period of a political party, he asserts was a major development.

This change in thinking among the Muslims from the older mode of dealing with the West, straightforward confrontation (usually military) to a newer one, dealing with the West using a Western tool, was striking. A political party was a device the Bosnian Muslims had never encountered, much less used, in their dealings with their former overlord, since throughout the hundreds of years of Ottoman rule, up to the occupation in

1878, no such thing had existed there, the first Ottoman parliament being convoked only at just this time.

To Bosnian Muslims, especially the less educated, at the time of the occupation, the idea that Austro-Hungarian society and norms represented a pattern possibly more technically advanced than their own would have been of little interest if they had thought about it. The significant difference for these people was that the Austrian empire was not a Muslim state, and so it was something to be resisted. One echo of this was an uncertainty that lingered for years as to whether Islam even allowed them to live in a non-Muslim state, not to mention serve it. However, no mention was found of any specific inquiry from the Bosnian Muslims to the religious authorities in Istanbul for a ruling on either the narrower issue of military service or the broader one of the acceptability for Muslims to live under non-Muslim rule, nor did the authorities in Istanbul volunteer one. One can only surmise that neither issue was raised that would have required of Ottoman jurists the characteristic, unqualified *olur/olmaz* (yes or no) answer because neither the Bosnian Muslims nor the Ottoman authorities were eager to have a difficult situation made impossible, given their weakness relative to Austria.

The forms in which the Bosnian Muslims expressed their identity in the Austrian period can be grouped into three categories: (1) traditional practice, e.g., participation in basic Muslim social or cultural institutions; (2) traditional forms with a new objective, e.g., local rebellions, but now against a Christian rather than Muslim ruler, or signing petitions of grievance against the authorities, again now Christian rather than Muslim; (3) entirely new forms, unprecedented in the Ottoman period, e.g., forming a political party. The first two were characteristic of political activism in the 1880s and early 1890s. The third emerged later in the 1890s, when the elite began actively to oppose Austrian rule.

The first instance of Muslim self-assertion came after the imminent Austrian occupation was announced. In July 1878, the Muslims took up arms and gathered around the mosques. One Hadji Lojo, a person with a somewhat checkered past, was chosen to head the resistance. The Ottoman government, clearly in no shape to resist the imminent Austrian demarche head on, sent a telegram to the Bosnians urging them to remain calm. Behind the scenes, however, the Ottomans backed a Bosnian protest to Bismarck against the Treaty of Berlin. After the Austrian proclamation of July 26 that they would be marching in, Austria waited for a sign that the Ottomans would help smooth the way for the occupation. The Ottomans made no such move. Angry Bosnians deposed the Ottoman *vali* and other Ottoman officials and chased the Austrian consul out of Sarajevo. At this point, Andrassy ordered the army into Bosnia.

On 3 August the Ottoman grand vizier called on the Bosnians to remain calm. To this the National Committee in Sarajevo responded with a message to the Ottomans: send no more advice. On 5 August the Austrian forces entered Mostar. The Muslims in Sarajevo now armed even foreign Muslims there and levied a tax on the Jews to aid the resistance. (In the Ottoman scheme of things, Jews never and Christians almost never bore arms but were liable instead to a special tax.)

By the middle of August, when the Austrian army arrived at Sarajevo, many of the Muslims had lost patience with the lawlessness of Lojo's group. Enough felt that those irregulars were a greater threat than the Austrians to allow much of the city to surrender; the small pockets of resistance were overcome in a few hours. By late October, the occupation was officially complete. A short-lived revolt in 1881–82 was also to some extent an expression of Muslim discontent, but it involved economic as well as political and religious motives and even some non-Muslims.

A cluster of issues involving Islam, Muslim practices, and

Muslim institutions was central if the Bosnian Muslims were to maintain their identity. Under the Ottomans they did not constitute a majority of the population, but their position as co-religionists of the ruling power had made them very strong. Now that they no longer enjoyed this advantage, they had several new concerns.

The first was conversion. Islam took a very dim view of any departure from Islam, seeing it as an act of apostasy, a betrayal entailing serious penalties, including the death penalty, although according to some, in the nineteenth century the Ottoman authorities in Bosnia had replaced the death penalty with banishment.

A second and related issue were the courts. As long as the Ottomans ruled Bosnia, the governmental authorities were also Muslim, and so whatever Muslim religious officials or courts decided to do with converts (or would-be converts) from Islam would be carried out. In this period, for the first, but not last, time the Bosnian Muslims faced the problem of dealing with conversion from Islam when the supreme secular authorities would not automatically support Muslim judges or courts. Accounts of the incidents that now provoked unrest often began with a case of conversion from Islam to Christianity, usually involving rather simple people, often young women. The central issue was, or was perceived to be, the survival of Islam, and that was important to all the Muslim population, irrespective of socioeconomic status. The human-interest side of these stories—which involved elements such as furtive love affairs, secret flights from authorities, and children hidden away—could easily engage the sympathies of even the least sophisticated elements of the Muslim population and the emotional appeal was a major factor in producing the flashpoint in these incidents.

The root of the problem was, however, the clash between the Muslim traditional and rigorous hostility to conversion, and the more tolerant Austrian view that any mature citizen was free to convert without incurring any legal penalty for doing so. The Austrian authorities wanted to treat the Muslims as the equals of the other religious groups. The Muslims, long accustomed to enjoying a higher position under Ottoman rule, continually resented this.

In 1878, at the beginning of Austrian rule in Bosnia, the government issued a directive to its officials urging them to keep their involvement in religious matters to a minimum. In the next year, in the Novi Pazar Convention with Turkey, the Austrians made several promises about respecting Islamic practices and allowing a religious connection with Ottoman authorities in Istanbul. These included such practices as the limited display of the Ottoman flag and continued reverence for the sultan's name. At this time there had been some other issues of a more abstract nature over which Muslims clashed with the Austrians, involving points of law or matters of almost exclusive concern to small groups of landholders. To address these issues the convention mentioned retaining the old social system, and finally— important to the landed gentry—a promise that government would make it clear to the local population, especially the peasants, that it did not intend to abolish the old order, only to ensure that laws were applied fairly everywhere.

In 1880, when the government presumably felt on somewhat firmer ground, it issued another directive, calling on its officials to act against anyone who violated the integrity of another's religion. The directive did not, however, come anywhere near to specifying in detail the proper course of action in a case of conversion or of a reaction to it. In 1881, in the Mostar area, a conversion occurred and very quickly the usual conflict of authorities emerged: the Austrians took the view that the young woman was of age and so free to convert, and the Muslims that it was a criminal act. The Muslims arrested her; the Austrians released her again and informed the sharia courts that they had no jurisdiction over such cases. The Muslim response was to petition the Austrian government about the conversion issue. It remained unresolved when a revolt connected with the new imposition of general military conscription upstaged the conversion problem.

This was yet another issue of Muslim identity: some Muslims opposed the draft on the grounds they were Ottoman subjects and should not be conscripted into a "foreign" army, a position perfectly intelligible in terms even of modern international law. Others objected because it was service in an infidel army. Still others fled: some 8,000 Bosnian Muslims emigrated to Turkey at this time.

In 1890 another dramatic case of conversion in Sarajevo brought that issue to the fore yet again, but since in this case the local archbishop became involved, the ramifications reached the higher levels of relations between the empire and Rome. As in the Mostar case, prominent Muslims in Sarajevo, including holders of some of the highest posts in civil and religious administration, signed petitions expressing concern over the danger posed to Islam by the event, and there was talk of sending a delegation to Vienna to present a petition directly to the emperor.

The next step toward resolution of the conversion issue appears to have owed much to a curious symbiosis that then developed between the Sarajevo Muslim elite and the local Austrian authorities. The former wanted, of course, to maintain under Austrian rule the privileged status they had enjoyed under the Ottomans, even though this now entailed a good bit of collaborating with the Austrian authorities. They also wished to hold onto their status as the true voice of the Muslim community to the Austrian authorities, which was more difficult. To succeed they would have to keep both a high degree of accord and unity among themselves, or at least the appearance of it, and their credibility with their coreligionists. The local Austrian authorities were of course aware that good relations with a Muslim elite made governing a much easier task. It was therefore not in the interest of the Austrian authorities to humiliate them by showing them to be powerless to defend the interests of the Muslims. Kallay in particular realized that the whole issue of conversion was inadequately covered by Austrian regulations.

From this conflict of views and interests emerged a compromise on conversion, with certain stipulations for legitimate conversion and with definite roles for the clergy of each religion involved. Although this embodied much of what the Muslims wanted, it did not fully satisfy them. Vienna continued to receive reports of Muslim discontent, until in 1891 it issued the Conversion Ordinance including new procedures for converts and government commissions to render final decisions in very conflicted cases. Although this compromise gave the Muslims some control over the process, it did not meet the wishes of the most conservative elements. The Sarajevo elite, however, had succeeded in maintaining its facade of unity and position vis-à-vis the Austrian authorities and to some extent vis-à-vis its Muslim coreligionists as well. Because the ordinance did not solve all aspects of the question, it left room for subsequent trouble, but it was nonetheless an important step in institutionalizing the encounter between Bosnian Islam and Christian Europe.

Incidents of conversion accompanied by confrontation continued, as did revisions of laws governing conversion over the years until the war. These changes suggest that even the Austrians were not fully satisfied with the solution.

While this struggle over the conversion issue was in progress, other developments began in Mostar, where the struggle over Islamic identity was becoming more complex. The activist forces there to some extent followed the Sarajevo pattern, but there were some significant differences. The Austrian imposition of universal military conscription was an issue of particular concern to poor Muslims. It had not been imposed immediately upon annexation, but in 1881 the Bosnian military units were incorporated into the imperial army, and it was introduced. Since service, however compulsory, in the Austrian army seemed illegal or treasonous to the masses, and wealthy Muslims were already discontented over Austrian property laws and other administrative regulations, the local revolt of 1881–82 flared briefly. After the Austrians had firmly suppressed it, there were several years of relative Muslim inactivity.

Late in 1881 the Austrians had sent an inspector to the area after discontent over conscription had first become a problem. He prepared an extensive report with recommendations based on his observation that the Muslims were divided into pro- and anti-Austrian camps. Government policy, he said, should be based on assisting and rewarding its friends. This policy was significant in the subsequent development of Muslim organizations.

Kallay, when he came to Sarajevo in 1882 to begin his term as joint finance minister, tried a unifying rather than dividing approach to elicit loyalty by attempting to introduce an official Bosnian nationality, to which all the religious groups of the province would belong and which would separate them from the Serbs. If successful, the idea would have solved several problems for the Austrian administration. First and foremost, it would have been an obstacle to South Slav unity. He tried, for example, to have the local language called *Bosnian,* but in the absence of any common basis in real historical experience of any of the groups in Bosnia, the notion never took hold. Another of his innovative policies to check ethnic controversy was to prohibit the use of ethnic or religious designations in the names of institutions. (When his successors abandoned this policy, such institutions as the Muslim Central Bank for Bosnia and Herzegovina in Sarajevo could be created.)

In 1884 the Austrian administration appointed as mufti for Mostar one Ali Džabić, who enjoyed high esteem both as a savant and person of great integrity. While in his political views he was not an outspoken advocate of military resistance to Austrian rule, a point noted by some Austrian observers, his conservative Muslim views led him to consider Austrian rule to be fundamentally incompatible with Islam and to some extent an intrusion of an alien entity, which was to be endured for a presumably finite period. He and some of his followers were convinced that the Koran forbade Muslims to serve a foreign power, so that even though he was inclined to a kind of political quietism, he and his followers were soon on a collision course with the Austrian administration.

The Mostar Muslim wealthy class included a much higher proportion of merchants than did the analogous group in Sarajevo, and this meant less dependance on income from peasants working the land. Accordingly, the cardinal economic grievance of the Sarajevo elite—namely, that Austrian policies allowed, if not encouraged, peasants to avoid paying the landlords the traditional taxes—was less burdensome for the Mostar rich and appears to have figured less prominently in their petitions in the early 1880s to the Austrian government. Instead, these petitions contained a mix of economic and religious grievances. The Mostar Muslims complained that while under the Ottoman system, tax records had been accessible so that one could easily see how much one might be in arrears; under Austrian rule, the process was long and awkward. They asked for more representation for Herzegovina on the provincial council, which was essentially dominated by the Sarajevo wealthy class. They claimed that the new court system was slow and inefficient.

Some of the demands had also an ethnic quality to them. The petitioners protested the dismissal of Ottoman officials from government service and the replacement in sharia courts of Turkish with the Bosnian language. Of a more straightforward religious nature were claims that Christians were desecrating

Islamic sites and that government policy, by not vigorously prosecuting the offenders, was in fact encouraging this.

Discussions and maneuverings during the rest of the 1880s, although not apparent then, in retrospect appear to have been the beginning of a chain of events that was to lead to the creation, some thirty years later, of a Muslim national political party.

In the mid-1890s, another prominent local Muslim, Mujaga Komadina, not a cleric and a somewhat more progressive thinker, challenged the hegemony of Džabić by trying, in 1896–97, to establish a society for more progressive ideas, to be called the *Kiraethane* (officially the Muslim Reading and Benevolent Society in Mostar). This was an institution common in many parts of the Eastern Mediterranean (in Turkish, *kiraathane*); it was essentially a teahouse where men would gather to drink tea, chat, and, if they could, read the papers. Komadina's vision went well beyond this to include a lecture series and creation, by the contributions of members, of a fund to assist needy students and make loans to deserving artisans. Komadina had also some broader ideas about revitalizing the cultural and educational life of his fellow Muslims and advocating certain reforms. Because of its moderate character, the idea appealed to the Austrian authorities as a possible counterforce to some local Serbian anti-Austrian agitation.

In the Muslim community, however, a struggle soon emerged between the more conservative Džabić and the more reformist Komadina. In the process ideological lines began to blur; most of the Muslims were fairly conservative and so Komadina's people, to increase their following, moved to the right. Some of the new features included the display of a kind of Islamic flag, the use of Turkish exclusively for official written communications to members and of Bosnian exclusively for communication with the Austrians, and possible publication in Mostar of a

Turkish newspaper. This flurry of concern for Turkish did not last long, since soon after another faction emerged that questioned why Turkish was being used when most of the members neither read nor spoke it. It also made the society somewhat less attractive to the Austrian authorities, who began to incline more toward reconciling the two factions rather than assisting one to dominate the other. They were not inclined to suppress the organization completely since they hoped to use it to make controlling the Muslims easier.

The shift to the right was given added impetus by another dramatic conversion-and-flight episode in 1899. One Austrian official, in an attempt to exculpate the Austrian authorities and incline the Muslims more toward reformist ideas, contended that since the Muslim schools were in such sorry shape, their inadequately educated pupils were easy prey for proselytizing. The steering body of the *Kiraethane,* the Committee of Twelve, now moved into new waters by going beyond simply protesting the failings of the Austrian administration to discussing plans for an overall restructuring of the administration of their schools and vakifs, which, since the Austrian occupation, were ultimately under Austrian control.

Another new element in this program was that of local control—a clear expression of resentment of the Sarajevan Muslim domination by Herzegovinians who clearly considered themselves their equals. This contributed to the conflict with the Austrians who tended to see Herzegovina as lower in status than Bosnia. Again there was talk of playing the Ottoman card, appealing to Istanbul if Vienna was not helpful. These developments and the Austrian rejection of this reform package helped to reconcile the two Muslim factions. The upshot of all of this was, according to Donia, that "the limits of personal networks gave way to the dynamics of a corporate entity."

In 1900, there were a series of meetings of Muslim notables from all over Bosnia and Herzegovina to plan strategy and widen the program. Several acts of the Austrian authorities only added impetus to the Muslim movement: Džabić was dismissed as mufti, the *Kiraethane* was suppressed, and the 1899 petition was rejected.

Again there was talk of the Ottoman card, this time in the form of asking the Ottomans to appoint a special commissioner for Bosnia as they had for other regions no longer under full Ottoman control such as Eastern Rumelia in Bulgaria. A more massive response to the setback was the emigration to Turkey in 1900 of some 7,000 Bosnian Muslims.

The struggle moved to a new level in 1900, when Džabić and some associates invited other Muslims to join them in Budapest and representatives of all regions came. They set up a permanent office there, with two members of their committee and a Hungarian clerk, one of whose more unusual jobs was to scan newspapers and translate relevant articles into Bosnian. The delegates explored contacts with Hungarian parliamentary groups but rejected an offer that if Bosnia would agree to become Hungarian crown land, all the rights the Austrians had not granted would be granted to the Muslims. The delegates also hired a lawyer to refine their draft statute to protect things Islamic in Herzegovina.

One conflict remained unresolved. Džabić was a cleric and concerned primarily with religious issues important to clerics and average people. More members of the group came from the landholding class. In earlier petitions of the 1880s this clash of interests had had limited importance because the petitions had mainly been responses to conversion incidents. Religious grievances predominated, with landholder, special-interest claims simply tacked on at the end. The last major petition in this series in December 1900, however, included a number of new points that were to become staples of the Muslim agenda for the next decade: Austria in 1879 had guaranteed Muslims unimpeded contact with religious authorities in Istanbul; since

Islam was a state religion, the Austrians, by depriving Islam of its dominant position in political life and society, were undermining it. Since under Austrian rule, Islamic institutions such as schools and vakifs were under Austrian officials, not Muslim control, an unacceptable situation had been created: the lords' control over the peasantry and over taxes and other privileges was weakened. To reform this situation Muslim institutions had to be put under the control of boards or officials selected by local Muslims or by groups they elected. Any conflict between state law and Islamic law as to be decided by the şeyhülislam in Istanbul, the highest Islamic judicial official of the Ottoman empire.

The authors of this new petition elaborated a series of arguments to win the support of various groups: simple peasants, the better educated, and of course, the landholders. The quantitative difference became qualitative: while earlier petitions had had hundreds of signatures, this time there were thousands. The government attempted to mobilize loyalists to produce counterpetitions and to break their solidarity, but this only spurred the petitioners to greater efforts. In the face of this, at the end of 1900 Kallay agreed to accept the petition and respond to it by February 1901.

The Muslims, who thought they had won, were then astonished when Kallay's response was to reject their demands. Since one of his main concerns was to do nothing that "could lead to the creation of a Muslim nation" in Bosnia-Herzegovina, he could accept neither a structure of Islamic institutions that would be under only the most minimal Austrian control nor the legal involvement of the şeyhülislam in the affairs of the Muslims. To prevent an explosion, the Austrians engaged in temporizing measures, negotiations, and attepts to wean away parts of the Muslim front not only with familiar goodies such as trade concessions but also new ones such as the possibility of scholarships to study in Germany.

The Muslim front, however, held. The Austrians then developed a new weapon against the emerging Muslim leadership in the form of the "illegal emigrants" ruling of October 1901. When activists traveled outside Bosnia, they were declared illegal emigrants and subject to immediate arrest on their return. In 1902 Džabić and some associates went to Istanbul on a visit and were declared illegal emigrants. They thus lost control in Bosnia, and the Turkish factor was greatly reduced because in Istanbul the Balkan guests were kept in suitable quarters but under a kind of house arrest. The government of Abdul Hamid wanted to prevent their coming into contact with revolutionary groups such as the Young Turks, but this treatment made it clear to the Bosnians that the Ottomans would not intervene in or for Bosnia in any significant way.

The Muslim forces were in shock and disarray over Kallay's rejection and Džabić's isolation in Istanbul. Džabić refused to give his blanket approval to the work of the committee at home, fearing that the landholders would assume control and replace Islamic concerns with their own economic agenda, so they could do nothing.

Then in 1903 Kallay died. He was replaced as joint minister of finance by a diplomat named Burian, who realized that Kallay's policy of trying to isolate Bosnia from the growing conflict in the Balkans was unworkable. He therefore began to encourage groups willing to concentrate on politically acceptable activities, which made it easier for the Muslims to engage in various kinds of organization building. One significant example of this was the creation, in 1903, of the benevolent, self-help, self-improvement society, Gajret, by some Muslims who had had contact with analogous societies of other ethnic groups. The actual founding after over a year of planning, drafting of documents, etc., came at a very propitious time for the kinds of activity Gajret wanted to engage in. Made up of members of the modernist wing of the community, it wanted to popularize and increase acceptance of certain Western achievements among the Bosnian Muslims. Clearly connected with this were its educational activities, which included pushing for modernization of the curriculum and aiding deserving students. On a very practical level, it sought to improve artisan training; as part of this effort, connections were developed not only with a local Muslim artisan association, but also with a Serbian economic development society in Belgrade. It published journals in which new ideas could be aired. This society continued to function until 1941, long after Austrian rule ended, and has been credited with producing a segment of the Bosnian Muslim intelligentsia.

The new, apparently conciliatory, wind brought in 1905 a new regulation for church and school autonomy, which might have reduced Muslim discontent had it not also called for a new tax to pay for the schools. This generated so much resentment that it ended the period of inactivity: in 1906 Džabić gave his blessing to the landholder leadership at home to act in his absence. In December 1906 a political party, the Muslim National Organization, was officially established with a party newspaper and a party program. The landholders had come to understand that to mobilize broad popular support, they had to frame issues—even essentially selfish concerns such as retaining control over peasants—in Islamic terms.

With an actual political party, the Muslims had an institutional structure to use in negotiations for cultural autonomy. In 1908 Serbian and Croatian parties were also founded, and their existence gave the Muslim party new clout as a balance tipper. The final annexation of Bosnia by Austria and the lack of Ottoman reaction to it meant that concern over Turkish involvement essentially vanished. A regulation was passed giving the Muslims a good deal of local control and legal recourse to the şeyhülislam. In 1910 the Muslims officially accepted the Austrian annexation and swore allegiance to the empire. A new Bosnian parliament was created in which the Muslims were represented along with the other national parties. By giving the wealthy Muslim landholding class the right to vote, which many of their coreligionists did not have, and seats in parliament, the Austrian government thought to bind them more closely to the empire. The parliament had ninety-two members—twenty of them ex officio and seventy-two elected; a complicated system of economic and other criteria guided eligibility for suffrage. Of the seventy-two elected, the Muslims had twenty-four, the Orthodox thirty-one, the Catholics sixteen, and the Jews one.

The new Muslim party very quickly learned the rules of the game and was soon in the middle of negotiations with the Serbian and Croatian parties, bargaining with their swing votes over divisive issues such as peasant emancipation, suggesting not only that they were ripe for this kind of political life but that the Austrians had been correct to involve them in the local political process. The party initiated a complex relationship among the Austrian authorities, Bosnian landholders, Muslim clerics, and the general Muslim population. The landholders had a list of issues on which they wanted the Austrians to act—several that involved maintaining parts of the old Islamic order that was to their advantage (e.g., payment to the landlords of some traditional taxes) but that had little appeal to ordinary Muslims or Muslim clerics, who organized fairly quickly around purely religious issues and established a movement that ultimately became far more powerful than the small size of the original groups would have suggested.

The advent of the Balkan Wars some two years later produced such upheavals in the parliament that the government disbanded it in July 1912 and again in May 1913. The severe defeats the Ottomans suffered and the gains of the Christian Balkan powers understandably pushed Muslim opinion in the direction of loyalty to Austro-Hungary. How much this new political constellation could have done toward amicably resolving ethnic disputes in Bosnia will remain forever a mystery, since after the assassination of Franz Ferdinand in Sarajevo in 1914 the Bosnian parliament was adjourned—as it turned out—forever.

ECONOMIC DEVELOPMENT:
ANALGESIC FOR ETHNIC CONFLICT?

One of the more intriguing possibilities for the zones of ethnic conflict in the Balkans on which I have been working for some time is that a rise in the standard of living might lower the level of violence. For example, the kind of violence one sees now in poor areas in Eastern Europe or the Caucasus is unlikely to erupt between the linguistic groups of Belgium or the region of Trieste. When one has a substantial part of the pie, one is less likely to be interested in destroying the pie plate, not to mention the kitchen. In areas of mixed ethnicity, there exists often an almost irresistible temptation to blame high unemployment, a high cost of living, and low wages on some scapegoat, and this often leads to, or intensifies, ethnic and religious conflict.

This section, then, engages in historical analysis but does so under the impact of current developments, which somehow underline a recurrent hypothetical in the former Yugoslavia: what would things be like if Austrian, rather than Ottoman domination, had, for a longer period, extended south of Croatia to include other areas, such as Serbia and Bosnia? Finding a test for a historical hypothetical—what if x or y had happened instead of what we know to have happened—is rare. However, in the period from 1878 to about 1912, when first the Balkan wars and then World War I broke out, Austria did administer another piece of the former Yugoslavia, and it provides a partial test. From an admittedly 1990s perspective, one wonders whether Austrian rule produced a significant increase in economic development in those forty years or at least helped Bosnia-Herzegovina move onto a development track toward economic well-being that would defuse racial and religious conflict. If not, why not, is a question of both historical and contemporary interest.

A certain amount of economic development took place under Austrian rule, but the question is whether this was the result of random investments or a conscious policy to foster economic development as a means of achieving political goals. One factor making for ambiguity on this point is that there were competing voices in the Austrian administration. Some wanted the area to flourish to ensure the permanence of the new acquisition to use as a stepping stone for further expansion in the Balkans, whereas others had not wanted even the additional Slavic population brought by this annexation, not to mention future additions.

This dilemma over investment was not a new one in the nineteenth-century colonization of former Ottoman lands. In the early 1820s in the newly established Russian administration in Bessarabia, some officials had wanted to make the new colonial zone a show place to attract additional Balkan Christians. But this objective was not favored by a majority of the Russian administration, which meant that the policy was implemented only partially, as the subsequent history of the region and Balkan emigration to southern Russia was to show. In the Austrian clash of policy, the most prominent advocate of the positive view, Kallay, the longest-tenured joint finance minister and Austrian administrator of Bosnia (1882–1903), wanted to foster economic development by improving transportation, expanding exploitation of natural resources, and encouraging industrial development. As a justification for a prosperous Bosnia, he argued that "a satisfied population was the best guarantee" for continued Austrian control of the area; only by "raising the living standard in Bosnia-Herzegovina could Austria hope to keep open the only door which she still had for commercial, cultural, and eventually political expansion." Others, much less enthusiastic, worked against the kind of commitment this would have required.

Some of the literature on Bosnia during this forty-year period reveals earlier conventional positions: some assumed that because Austria had a higher level of development than the Ottoman state, Austrian rule automatically brought certain benefits; others assumed almost equally automatically that the large empire and the small new province must have shared a relationship of imperialist exploitation. Some of the newer literature is less inclined to support either view. John Lampe (1982), a leading specialist on the economic history of the Balkans, pointed out that some analyses of economic development in the Habsburg periphery "suggest that the relatively greater industrial development in the northern Habsburg regions would push ahead agricultural production in these southern and eastern borderlands. Conversely, the absence of modern industry elsewhere in the Ottoman empire should have opened the way for manufacturing" in certain areas in the Balkans. Utilizing "both sets of scholarship and scattered statistical data," he reached "some rather surprising conclusions." One was that agricultural production did not increase significantly in response to the new, broad, imperial market, as he discovered by comparing agricultural statistics from Austrian-controlled territory with statistics from Ottoman Macedonia and independent Romania. Another was that under Austro-Hungarian rule, industry in some areas of the Balkans—not apparently including Bosnia-Herzegovina—did register advances, but Lampe points out that these require more detailed analysis than simply linking them with "the general trend toward agricultural stagnation and industrial development."

The fine points of this discussion need not concern us here, but the question of "agricultural stagnation" is crucial since the overwhelming majority of the population continued to be engaged in agriculture. Much of the land in Bosnia-Herzegovina was and still is not particularly fertile. Accordingly, substantial increases in agricultural productivity and in personal incomes could come only from significantly advancing the technology of agriculture to increase production and from major advances in communications to provide cheaper and more rapid means of getting products to markets outside the province. The other significant alternative for raising the level of prosperity would have entailed a substantial shifting of population from small-scale agriculture to new industries and a subsequent reorganization of agriculture into more efficient large-scale units. These last two transformations would have required significant infusions of capital into these provinces, not to mention substantial changes in the mentality of both the wealthy and poor. Although there are indications that more capital was available and its manipulation became easier in the empire in the later nineteenth century, neither of these transformations occurred on any great scale in Bosnia-Herzegovina in the period under consideration.

A potentially significant factor in increasing exports and income in the agricultural sector and then in creating and expanding the industrial sector was the railroad. The story of the railroads cannot be given here in detail, but aspects of this story are relevant for understanding what happened, and did not happen, in other industrial sectors.

Earlier in the 1870s European capital had built rail lines in Serbia, Macedonia, and a link to Istanbul. Some railroad lines were constructed in Bosnia, such as the line from Brod to Sarajevo, but certain potentially key lines—from Sarajevo to an Adriatic port and to a link with the line to Istanbul—were not built. There were several factors in play here: instability, political and financial, in the Balkan region and in the Ottoman empire supplied a continuous background obligato above which, by fits and starts, some European investment took place. If foreign investment was so problematic, a government interested in the economic and noneconomic (e.g., strategic) aspects of railroads might be expected to step in, disregarding the risks that deterred other investors. Kallay, interested in railroad development, hoped for support from the military. In fact, the first line built (just before he took office), from the Hungarian border at Brod to Zenica, was built by the army. This project, however, was rather cheap and simple because the distance was short, the terrain easy, and narrow-gauge single track and army labor were used.

But the ultimate imperial authority, the Joint Finance Ministry in Vienna, was not interested in heavy investment. A law from 1880 required that Bosnia was to cover all its own costs from its own revenue. In Hungarian circles there was an interest in preventing the emergence of competition in Bosnia. Kallay used several tactics for dealing with the shortage of investment capital. One kind of creative financing that he borrowed from his predecessor and used repeatedly was to tap imperial common credits for his province through the Joint Commission, which was outside the control of the Austrian and Hungarian parliaments. The other was to encourage and reward investors by making secret concessions to them. Some criticized his means but none his ends, and so the government tolerated his tactics.

After Kallay's death, his successor Burian rejected his approach and did not extend concessions or grant new ones. (Some of the initial concessions, however, were so long term that they were still in force in 1918.) Not surprisingly, there was no massive influx of state capital to fill the new gap. The result was an economic slowdown and the conversion of some private enterprises to state enterprises. The latter took place in a syndrome readily intelligible to Americans today—debtors holding the whiphand on their creditors—with the variation here that concessionaires, facing nonrenewal of the favorable terms of the concession, told government officials that without those breaks they could not stay in business. The government, apparently in the face of possible negative consequences from closure of the enterprise, became directly involved. The economic engine of the Austrian empire, at least in Bosnia, appears to have lost much of its energy in what in another discipline would be called "internal friction."

The Austrian development of the road system was significant and in some respects an interesting counterexample to the case of the railroads. Sugar (1963) observed that this network was well planned and executed and kept within the budgetary capacity of the province by the use of corvée labor. He concluded with a sophisticated evaluation of this policy: such a practice was socially regressive, but it was the only way then possible to achieve certain economic goals.

Most of the population was engaged in agriculture, and here, as in most of the Balkans, a shortage of agrarian credit was a continuous problem. The Austrians made an attempt to alleviate this by creating agrarian credit operations in each of the forty-one districts. Funds were inadequate to meet the needs of all, and as it became clear that loans were going mainly to those in the good graces of the local authorities, peasants began creating their own operations. Over two hundred were created in this period. As for commercial credit, throughout the period there were many openings and closings by banks from elsewhere in the empire. The Muslim Central Bank for Bosnia and Herzegovina in Sarajevo was opened. But banks from other parts of the empire never became involved in major development efforts, and no local banking system capable of doing this emerged.

The issue of peasant indebtedness was connected with that of religious divisions by the fact that many nonfree peasants were Christian and all landlords were Muslim. The *kmets* were, as we have seen, subject to heavy obligations to local lords under the Ottomans, and many Christian *kmets* clearly expected that under a Christian government they would be freed from them. When this did not happen, the *kmets* began refusing to fulfill their obligations, which in turn led to complaints by

Muslim landlords to the Austrian authorities. The imperial government had several reasons for not meeting the expectations of the Christian peasants: tithes made up about a third of the revenue of the Austrian administration of Bosnia, which probably found it easier to leave collection structures in place. Expropriating the land of the Muslim landlords, probably the ultimate hope of the Christian peasants, would have been anathema to the landholding gentry of Hungary. When the Bosnian parliament finally came into being and the question of *kmet* obligations came up, the bargaining among the government and national parties included discussions of how to avoid massive emancipation, showing once more how involving the Muslim landlords in the government had ensured their loyalty. But it also put the imperial government in the position of defending a major interest of a few rich Muslims against the major interest of a significant part of the Christian population.

Austrian rule left the province with some significant physical assets (mainly railroad lines and roads), little in the way of an industrial base or adequate financial services, and the legacy of a customs duty policy that had been inappropriate for fostering economic growth. Much of the peasantry remained mired in low-productivity agriculture. Movement out of this was not an option for most of the peasants, both because those not yet emancipated could not move and because even for free peasants there was no new, rapidly expanding industrial sector to which they could relocate.

Another factor affecting economic growth and any attendant sense of well-being was the cost of the administration. Given the Austrian minimalist intervention policy in religious matters, one might have expected an equally minimalist position in administration. This was certainly not the case in Bosnia, as can be seen from a few statistics on growth of the administration from the end of the Ottoman period. According to Sugar (1963), when the Ottomans left Bosnia in 1878, they had about 120 officials there. The Austrians had some 600 by 1881, over 7,000 by 1987, and over 9,500 by 1908. Even if the 120 Ottomans were supplemented by additional Ottoman officials before trouble began in 1875 and by additional local Bosnians serving in the Ottoman administration, the bureaucracy that had run the country for several hundred years was nowhere near the size of the bureaucracy that by 1908 had been administering the territory for only thirty years.

While the Austrian administration took over some Ottoman structures, others were expanded. The dual nature of the monarchy created at the outset a problem of status for Bosnia: should Bosnia be in the Austrian half or the Hungarian half of the empire, or should it be directly under the crown? As Sugar pointed out, Austria followed the Ottomans; what had been owned directly by the Ottoman empire, the vilayet, became imperial land (*Reichsland*), and the earlier subdivisions were slotted into their Austrian counterparts, sanjaks became *Kreise* and *kaza*s became *Bezirke*.

The real difference came in the much more extensively branched Austrian administration. A political division handled some expected functions, such as some aspects of foreign relations and policing, and also controlled education, religious matters, and health. A financial division handled not only the predictable budget and customs office but also matters affecting industry, commerce, and transportation. There were other divisions for justice, forests, and mines, and records and accounting. Much of this was new to formerly Ottoman Bosnia, since Western-style ministeries with titles analogous to those of the West were not introduced into the Ottoman central government until the middle decades of the nineteenth century and in the provincial administration on an experimental basis only in the late 1860s with the creation of the model Tuna Vilayeti, or Danubian province, in nearby northern Bulgaria, an experiment that was not a total success.

One striking aspect of Austrian administration in Bosnia was the high level of qualification of a number of those appointed to head it, despite problems in finding appropriate people for some lower-level appointments. Benjamin Kallay, by the time of his appointment in 1882, had served in Belgrade for seven years in the Austrian foreign service, spoke fluent Serbian, wrote a history of the Serbs, and was considered to be a leading specialist on South Slav matters. Kallay's successor Burian also came to the task with considerable experience of Eastern Europe, having studied in Bratislava (as well as Vienna) and then served as a diplomat in Bucharest, Sofia, Moscow, and Belgrade. Bilinski, Burian's successor from Galicia, was a well-known professor of economics in Lvov, who had also held several high economic administrative posts. During his term (1912–1915), he made some administrative reforms but was unable to do much with the economy since there was, when he came in, a parliamentary crisis, soon followed by the Balkan Wars, soon followed by World War I. A more detailed history of the attempts of these high-level experts to surmount obstacles in other parts of the administration and deal with some rather intractable local problems would provide interesting cautionary tales.

It bears repeating here that even if some of the opposition to Austrian rule was based on religious or cultural grounds, there was also a solid material basis for it. In the Austrian scheme of things the province was obliged to cover all its administrative costs, which grew as the bureaucracy grew. Most of the new officials were not only not Muslims but not even Bosnians. Bosnian Muslims also complained that the imperial courts were much slower than the older Muslim courts. This slowness may at first glance be suspected of having been a ploy by the Muslim landowners to retain control, but when this situation is looked at in the larger context of development of Austrian administration a different picture emerges. According to Sugar, general Austro-Hungarian practice at this time had been to save money by abolishing lower levels of courts and referring the matters such courts would have handled to administrative officials. However, the delays this occasioned became apparent during the 1880s, and when the Austrians then recreated the lower-level courts, the situation improved substantially. While Austrian rule brought some economic benefits to the region, the forcible separation from the Ottoman empire had some negative costs for the Bosnians, especially the Muslims. The imposition of the Austrian customs system on the region ended Sarajevo's role as the main entrepôt for Ottoman goods entering the region. In view of the relative proportions of wealth and membership in the merchant class of Muslims and Christians, the losses were greater for the Muslims. Incorporation into the Austrian customs union, even though it was probably of limited duration, almost certainly weighed most heavily on some Muslims because it ended the acceptance of Ottoman money in circulation in Bosnia.

The requirement of service in the Austrian army was another source of discontent and not only to the Muslims. When the new conscription law was proclaimed even some of the Serbs in Mostar signed a petition reaffirming the sultan's authority there. The Austrian authorities were dumbfounded at this kind of Muslim-Orthodox cooperation, but the resistance was driven in part by the military service's heavy cuts in the labor available for agriculture and thereby their livelihood.

For success in economic development the administration had to provide, at a minimum, a modicum of stability and regularity, but for rapid economic development it would have had to contribute considerably more than this. Gains in organizational structure and in the creation of assets do not appear to have been sufficient either to overbalance the various political, religious, and other discontents or to facilitate achieving this shortly thereafter.

In an attempt to analyze Austria's role in this time and place, it is perhaps of interest that in historical evaluations of the Ottoman empire, some historians interested in defending that empire aganst some of its critics have advanced an argument that runs in general as follows: it is not proper to criticize the Ottoman state for not having addressed certain social, economic, or cultural problems as would a modern Western state, since Ottoman administrators did not see them as proper concerns of government. However much or little one may agree with this position it is impossible to reject it completely and to some extent the same line of thought is valid with regard to Austro-Hungarian rule.

BOSNIAN MUSLIMS AND THE TURKISH STATE

While the substance of the straightforwardly Islamic issues is fairly clear and the position of Bosnian Muslims to Islam unambiguous, the relationship between the Bosnian Muslims and the Turkish state is not so. The complexities of this relationship have historical as well as contemporary interest.

One obstacle for the would-be student of these attitudes is connected with a kind of continuation of Ottoman cultural traditions. In studying Ottoman attitudes and changes in attitudes, one quickly comes up against the almost total absence of first-person literature—diaries, collected letters, and autobiography—even from highly placed officials. (My attempt some years ago to find an explanation for this by asking a number of eminent Turkish historians why they thought this gap existed produced interesting speculation but no clear answer.) Not surprisingly, in our period, since the Bosnian notables of the Austrian period were largely products of that same culture, there is little such first-person literature from them either. Other indicators of attitudes available in studying other societies, such as editorials or articles in a periodical press, are also in short supply in studying the Bosnian Muslims.

Antagonism was apparent earlier in the nineteenth century when Ottoman officials had not been particularly welcome in Bosnia. The local Muslim lords preferred to run things themselves, so much so that the Ottoman government had to intervene militarily in the middle of the nineteenth century to reassert its control over the area. On the other side there were indications that Ottoman officials were not overly eager to serve there because it was considered a dull provincial backwater or because they were not interested in wrestling with local power brokers even after the reassertion of Ottoman control. Despite this, several Ottoman governors in the last two decades of direct Ottoman rule oversaw significant achievements in various fields such as public works and education.

After the Treaty of Berlin it appears most of the Ottoman officials left Bosnia, some voluntarily and some under pressure from Bosnian Muslims but, in all, a development welcome to the Austrians and not protested by the Muslims at that time. Possibly pro-Ottoman attitudes were exhibited over the next two decades, when the local Muslims called for retention of Ottoman officials or other links with Istanbul, involving appointment or confirmation of religious dignitaries. What does not emerge from the sources is whether this was out of loyalty to the Ottoman empire or mainly a product of such concern over their Islamic identity that they were willing to clutch at any straw.

Attachment to Ottoman Turkish varied, as has been seen, from group to group and at different times. The demand for retention of Turkish in the sharia courts suggests an essentially elite concern. Ottoman Turkish, a convoluted literary language, especially rich in Arabic and Persian loan words, was not understood by the lower classes in Turkey, not to mention the lower classes in Bosnia. It should also be remembered that the Turks had never pursued a policy of massive Turkification there, forcing or even encouraging Bosnians to learn Turkish or become

Turks in any significant sense. Only members of the Bosnian Muslim elite had learned Ottoman, either locally or through schooling in Istanbul.

This was manifested in our period when one of the motivations for the creation of a newspaper in Bosnian was that too few people could read the extant Turkish newspaper *Vatan*. Seen in this light, efforts to have Turkish retained appear to have a dual character: (1) as a significant element of the local Muslim historic identity and (2) as a mark of the special status of the elite, since whenever it would be used, simple folk, as well as Austrian officials, would have to work through an interpreter.

Turkey remained uniquely important for Bosnian Muslims throughout this period, however, as a place of refuge. This relationship also included conflicting attitudes. The emigration decline after peak periods of tension in Bosnia suggests that it was not considered an ideal or total solution to the problems of Bosnian Muslims under Christian rule.

Assessing satisfaction with the emigration option after one has initial emigration figures requires examination of three related emigration issues. The importance of these when analyzing such movements first became clear to me while working on analogous population movements around the Black Sea in the nineteenth century. The first of these issues we might call "emigré satisfaction." The emigrés' satisfaction with their new home balanced the advantages of no longer being a religious minority, at times persecuted, against the disadvantages, often economic, of starting life as a new immigrant. The second is statistical data on those who returned home shortly after emigrating as one indicator of dissatisfaction. In the absence of first-person literature, such statistics become all the more important. The statistical data on returnees were fragmentary. A few sources mentioned that some of those who fled in 1878 did return; one work mentioned that the first petition for a mass return recorded by the Austrian authorities was from 1912. The third factor needed to calculate the percentage of returnees is mortality among the emigrants. Again, earlier works on other Muslim migrations to the Ottoman empire suggest that the emigrants faced hardships that modern readers may not be aware of: the length of the trip in those days for all, added hardships for the poor, shortages of food and water along the way and in refugee centers, coupled with epidemics due to polluted water and little or no sanitation. All of these took their toll on the already weakened and reduced number of recent arrivals before they could be moved elsewhere for final relocation. In such chaotic situations of minimal sanitation and health measures, understandably no one was keeping statistics, and few such figures can be found. The recurrence of some of the problems encountered by Tatar and Circassian immigrants to the Ottoman empire in the mid-nineteenth century in accounts of the reception of large numbers of Bulgarian Turks in Turkey a few years ago suggests what some immigrants from Bosnia, in the larger waves, might have faced when the Turkish state, with very limited means at its disposal and no coordinated large-scale assistance from other Muslim states, had to deal suddenly with thousands of immigrants. In the absence of global or even more detailed partial figures, the degree of "emigré satisfaction" cannot be measured satisfactorily. It appears possible only to sketch the factors that would have influenced it.

While some of the wealthier emigrés presumably continued to live fairly well, according to one work the hardships for the group as a whole included a high mortality rate. Particularly disturbing to some of those who fled especially to preserve their Islamic identity, according to another study, was the absence of adequate educational opportunities for their children.

The complex of relationships between the Bosnian Muslims

and the Turkish state had a kind of whirling kaleidoscope character—a positive feature, the Islamic tie; a negative one, Ottoman centralization; appeals for help after the annexation was announced; disappointment with Ottoman inaction after this; Turkey as a safe haven; some disappointment encountered there; and so on.

As though all of this were not perplexing enough for the general reader, the literature on Bosnia presents differing and at times sharply conflicting evaluations of the Ottoman role. A little light on generational and related differences among scholars working on this area may be helpful. For example, Peter Sugar (1963), whose study of the industrialization of Bosnia-Herzegovina in the Austrian period is a major work on the history of Bosnia, was one of the earliest members of the group of post-1945 Balkanists whose training included much work on the Ottoman empire under a full-time specialist on Turkish history. The difference between Balkanists who studied the Ottoman empire from within and those who studied it only from without (from the perspective of the history of the neighboring Balkan states and through the work of their historians) has long been apparent to some in the profession but understandably is almost unknown outside of it. The former group, which I joined about a decade after Sugar, tends to take much more of an on-the-one-hand, on-the-other view of the character and functioning and legacy of the Ottomans in the Balkans. Earlier generations of Balkan specialists whose training did not include this, or specialists in Europe trained either in the other Balkan states or mainly on the literature produced in those states, tended to take a more negative view of this legacy. Expertise on the Balkans may resemble some beverages brewed in the area: what kind of tap you use and where in the vat you put the tap may affect what comes out.

The weighings and balancings on many points in this chapter have raised as many questions as they have answered. The reader who feels this may find some consolation in having moved to another level of understanding matters in the Balkans.

NOTES

1. Briefly put, this approach might be termed *ethnic calculus*—analyzing a situation in which several variables (the policies, tactics, etc., of ethnic local groups and the foreign states involved) are changing at the same time. Unlike mathematics, however, in this kind of analysis the earlier values of the variables have a greater importance for understanding the situation at whatever point in time it is being examined. This is admittedly more difficult than analysis dealing with only one side or one point in time, but then understanding ethnic conflict in the Balkans, or many other places, is rarely easy.

2. A primary goal of this conference was to present the historical background of the development of the Bosnian Muslims rather than address the immediate present situation—the last two years (since the formal dissolution of Yugoslavia) or the last year (since the beginning of the Bosnian war)—largely because those phases have already received much coverage, while the historical background had been largely ignored. The Center for Middle Eastern Studies approaches this whole subject primarily as a subset of Islamic studies, a discipline in which historical perspectives play a large role. All of the conference participants were by training and practice historians, not journalists or social scientists. However, historians also feel the strong pull of the present intense situation in Bosnia, moving some conference participants to highlight, in the course of their papers, certain aspects of the past, which in calmer times would be more simply inventoried. (For example, some twenty years ago, I wrote my dissertation on what I called then the "demographic war" for the Black Sea, analyzing forced/ "encouraged" population movements in the nineteenth century around the Black Sea, including areas then considered obscure but frequently in the headlines this past year (Pinson, 1970). Accordingly, I ask my fellow historians to be tolerant of some of the

observations we have made at this conference and not conclude that we are indulging in some sort of lese-majesty toward history.

3. One major element of the Bosnian national culture, the oral epic, owes much of its preservation to two Harvard scholars—Professor M. Parry in the 1930s, and his student and successor, Professor Albert Lord from after World War II until his recent death—who did much to gather and publish texts of Bosnian oral epics.

REFERENCES

Donia, Robert J. (1981). *Islam Under the Double Eagle: The Muslims of Bosnia and Herzegovina, 1878–1914.* East European Monographs, no. 78. Boulder: East European Quarterly. New York: Columbia University Press.

Dedijer, V., and M. Ekmecic, et al. (1974). *History of Yugoslavia.* New York: McGraw-Hill.

Lampe, John R. (1982). *Balkan Economic History, 1550–1950: From Imperial Borderlands to Developing Nations.* Joint Committee on Eastern Europe Publication Series, no. 10. Bloomington: Indiana University Press.

Pinson, Mark. (1970). "Demographic Warfare: An Aspect of Ottoman and Russian Policy, 1854–1866. Ph.D. dissertation, Harvard University.

Sked, Alan. (1989). *The Decline and Fall of the Habsburg Empire, 1815–1918.* New York: Longman.

Sugar, Peter F. (1963). *Industrialization of Bosnia-Herzegovina: 1878–1918.* Seattle: University of Washington Press.

Bosnian Muslims: From Religious Community to Socialist Nationhood and Postcommunist Statehood, 1918–1992

Ivo Banac

Yale University

There is a Bosnian Muslim story about a learned Frenchman who came to Istanbul and offered to convert to Islam should the sultan find somebody who could read the visitor's thoughts. After some prompting the sultan remembered Nasruddin Hoca, the fabled sage of Oriental lore, who was summoned to the Porte to try his hand at communication by pure thought. The Frenchman made a circle with his hand and Nasruddin signaled vertically as if to split the circle. The Frenchman lowered his hand and wiggled his fingers. Nasruddin raised his hand and did the same. The Frenchman was startled and produced an egg from his pocket. Nasruddin responded by offering a lump of cheese from his. The Frenchman jumped to his feet and acknowledged Nasruddin's ability to read his mind. "Now make me a Turk as best as you know," he concluded.

The sultan asked the Frenchman to explain his "conversation" with Nasruddin. "I made a circle," he responded, "as if to say, the earth is round. He cut it in half, as if to say, one half is water. I signaled from below, as if to say, all kinds of plants grow from the soil. He signaled from above, thereby pointing out that rains falls from above and makes growth possible. I reached for my egg, as if to say, the earth is like this. He produced a piece of cheese, as if to say, this is how it looks when it snows."

As the Frenchman departed, the sultan congratulated Nasruddin and asked him to tell his side. "That was easy," said the Hoca. "He made a circle, as if to say, I have a good loaf. I eagerly responded by suggesting that we split it evenly. He signaled from below, as if to say, I also have good pilaf. And I signaled from above, as if to say, grease it well. He offered an egg, suggesting that we shall also bake a *çılbır* (egg dish). And I showed a lump of cheese, as if to say, we shall also make sauce." The sultan laughed and rewarded Nasruddin. "Since that time," the story concludes, "it is said: They understood one another like Nasruddin Hoca and the Frenchman (Frndić, 1972, 122).

"Make me a Turk!" The Ottoman conquest of Bosnia, which was completed under Mehmed the Conqueror (Fatih) and Bayezid II, from 1463 to 1482, brought Islam into the religiously divided kingdom of Bosnia. From the thirteenth century, this land was hospitable to the dualist sect—the church of Bosnia, probably a blend of Catholic church organization and neo-Manichean doctrine, but not identical, even in name, to the Bulgarian Bogomils, as is frequently and erroneously asserted. This was the church of the Bosnian majority, powerful both at the court and among the people. But its heretical reputation, which was magnified by Bosnia's canonical Christian neighbors, occasioned frequent interventionist crusades, especially from Catholic Hungary-Croatia.[1] Since the Catholic West was the only possible source of aid against the Turks, the influence of the Catholic church, notably of the Franciscan order, grew on the eve of the conquest.[2] The last kings of Bosnia were Catholics who promoted Franciscan piety in the heart of old Bosnia.

Simultaneously, on the eastern fringes of Bosnia and especially in the Transnarentan Hum (modern eastern Herzegovina), which Bosnia subjoined in the fourteenth century, the Orthodox monasteries continued their ministry.[3]

The conquest mixed the cards but did not extirpate the older religious communities. The Ottomans assumed the superiority of Islam, but—unlike their European Christian contemporaries—they did not try to bring the other monotheistic religions into their fold by force. (It never would have occurred to Bayezid II to expel the Christians or Jews from his realm.) The millet system preserved the Christian churches in Bosnia and with them the potential for national heterogeneity. Nevertheless, it is assumed—and occasionally documented—that the adherents of the church of Bosnia acceded to Islam, thereby prompting a rare (for the Balkans) mass conversion to the "Turkish faith." To be sure, conversion to Islam did not entirely bypass the Catholic and Orthodox communities, but Islamization was apparently much less frequent among the canonical Christians than among the neo-Manichean sectaries. Further, the Ottoman conquest prompted vast migrations of peoples. Catholics fled to Habsburg Croatia, the Venetian possessions on the littoral, and beyond. Their deserted hearths frequently were taken by Orthodox Balkan Vlachs, who by this time were fully Slavonicized.[4] Moreover, remaining Catholics often acceded to Eastern Orthodoxy, a faith that was less likely to be persecuted on account of subversion than Catholicism, whose temporal head, the pope, was not only beyond the Ottoman reach—unlike the patriarch of Constantinople—but actively participated in, and frequently was the initiator of, anti-Ottoman crusades.[5]

When the Turks—actually mainly Slavic Bosnian Muslims—withdrew from Hungary and Croatia before the advancing Habsburg and Venetian forces in the course of the War of the Holy League (1683–99), thereby initiating a century of Ottoman retreat from Central Europe and the Adriatic basin, Bosnia became predominantly Islamic.[6] Muslim percentages increased with the Ottoman retreat from autonomous Serbia and Montenegro in the early nineteenth century, but steadily decreased in the three migratory waves (mainly to Turkey) that followed the Congress of Berlin and the Austro-Hungarian occupation of Bosnia-Herzegovina (1878), the establishment of the Yugoslav state (1918), and the Communist takeover (1945).

It is important to note here a change in European sensibility that transpired between the Peace of Carlowitz (1699), which completed the construction of Bosnia's western borders, and the Congress of Berlin. When Eugene of Savoy burned Sarajevo to the ground in 1697, intolerance in religious matters was the accepted European practice. No functioning mosque was permitted to stand in the liberated portions of Hungary and Croatia. Intolerant attitude, too, marked the Balkan national revolutions. Belgrade, once a city of myriad mosques, today has one. How many functioning mosques remain in Sofia, Salonika, and Bucharest? This means that there would be no Bosnian Muslims today had Eugene of Savoy held on to Bosnia in the late seventeenth century, or had Serbian insurgent Karadjordje extended his uprising into Bosnia after 1804. But when General Josef Freiherr von Philippovich led the Austro-Hungarian troops into Bosnia in the summer of 1878, the time for mosque burning and "religious cleansing" was over. Balkan developments always lagged behind Europe. Muslim Albanians were obliged to flee Kuršumlija in 1878 after Serbia expanded into the four southern districts of Niš, Pirot, Toplica, and Vranje. But when the Serbians moved into Kosovo in 1912, they were no longer pursuing the goal of a pure Orthodox Christian state. Similarly, the existence of a Muslim minority in Bulgaria—both Bulgarian (Pomak) and Turkish—speaks to the lateness of the Bulgarian national state. This is why the current "ethnic cleansing" in Bosnia, attended by the destruction of mosques (90 percent of which were destroyed in Serb-held parts of Bosnia), represents a cultural reversion to pre-Enlightenment ideational modes.

Bosnian Muslims identified with the Ottoman state but were always fully aware that they were not Anatolians. There is a story about a Bosnian *sîpahî* (squire) who was offended by a *hatib* (preacher) of a leading Istanbul mosque. The *hatib*'s Friday sermon was full of references to Arabs and Acems (Persians, non-Arabs) but contained no mention of Bosnians. Called to account, the *hatib* noted that the term Acem covered the Bosnians. All the same, when during his next sermon he saw the *sîpahî* reach for his sword as he mentioned only the Arabs and Acems, he quickly added *"vel Bošniakati"*—"and the Bosnians, too" (Salihagić, 1940, 20).

In the Ottoman days Bosnian Muslims called themselves either Turci, as opposed to Turkuše (Anatolian Turks), or Bošnjaci (Bosnians). They referred to their language as Bošnjački (Bosnian) and wrote it both in Arabic script or in Bosančica (the Bosnian or Croatian recension of Cyrillic script) (Hadžijahić, 1974, 15–31). The latter was also used by Bosnian Franciscans, who were the real guardians of Bosnian state traditions under the Turks.

Bosnian Islam was no more latitudinarian than the Islam of the Ottoman empire, but it always reached for an authenticity that was inevitable in frontier areas.[7] The unsuccessful uprising of Husein-kapetan Gradščević against the Porte (1831) was prompted not only by hostility to the reforms of Mahmud II, but also by the Porte's territorial concession to Serbia, and unwillingness to protect the Muslims of Obrenović Serbia. After the Austro-Hungarian occupation in 1878, Bosnian Islam became quite tame, integrated as it was within the etatist policy of the Habsburg monarchy toward the non-Catholics.[8] Though the Catholic church certainly thrived in Habsburg Bosnia, it cannot be claimed that it was privileged or that the other religious communities were neglected.[9] The secularization of Bosnian Muslims continued throughout the Habsburg and Yugoslav periods, permitting the Serb-Croat rivalry over Bosnian Muslim "nationalization"—that is, the attempts to convince the Muslims that they did not constitute a separate national group and that it was "progressive" to choose between the Serb and Croat national identities. For its part, the Austro-Hungarian administration discouraged Bosnia's links with Croatia and fostered specifically Bosnian national sentiment (bošnjaštvo) (Kraljačić, 1987). Though the Muslim intelligentsia overwhelmingly thought of itself as Croatian, most Bosnian Muslims avoided taking sides between the two Christian communities, feeling that the demands for their "nationalization" undermined Muslim unity.

During the interwar years, after the establishment of Yugoslavia in 1918, the Serb community of Bosnia-Herzegovina became an instrument of Serbian hegemony, which was resisted by Croats and Muslims.[10] The predominant Muslim party of the period—the Yugoslav Muslim Organization (JMO)—fought for the autonomy of Bosnia-Herzegovina, which it defended even at the price of collusion with the Belgrade regimes. In March 1921, the JMO departed from its program and entered into an agreement with the ruling coalition of Nikola Pašić's Radical party (Great Serbian nationalists) and Ljubomir Davidović's Democratic party (Yugoslavist unitarists). The price was the government's promise to promote the equality of Islam, the autonomy of Muslim religious-educational institutions and sharia courts, lenient application of agrarian reform, and, most important, the maintenance of Bosnia-Herzegovina's historical borders and territorial integrity in internal administrative arrangements (Purivatra, 1974, 128). In exchange, the JMO's twenty-three deputies in the Constituent Assembly voted for the government's centralist constitutional proposal on 28 June 1921, thereby assuring the victory of the centralist bloc. Without these votes and those of eight additional deputies of the Cemiyet, an allied autonomist party of Bosnian, Albanian, and Turkish Muslims of the Sanjak, Kosovo, Metohia, and Macedonia, the centralist Vidovdan constitution would not have been adopted (cf. Banac, 1984, 402–4).

Instead of keeping its part of the bargain, the Pašić government delayed the implementation of promises to the JMO. When King Aleksandar issued a Decree on the Division of the Country into Districts on 26 June 1922, the outer shell of Bosnia-Herzegovina was preserved by way of maintaining the old Austro-Hungarian districts (Bihać, Banja Luka, Tuzla, Travnik, Sarajevo, Mostar), but Bosnia-Herzegovina was no longer a reality. Indeed, of the six Bosnian-Herzegovinian district chiefs (*veliki župani*) not a single one was a Muslim. This led to upheavals within the JMO. The younger and more disgruntled group of JMO deputies, the so-called leftists, led by Dr. Mehmed Spaho (1883–1939), increasingly opted for an oppositional course and cooperation with the Croat parties. The older and more conservative group of rightists, led by Hadji Hafiz Ibrahim efendi Maglajlić, the mufti of Tuzla and the JMO's first president, insisted on relying on the government and the Serbian parties. In October 1921 Spaho prevailed at the JMO's main assembly and was elected the party's president. He resigned from his post of minister of trade and industry in the Pašić cabinet in February 1922. The Maglajlić group, however, retained two cabinet posts in the reconstructed Pašić cabinet and evolved into a separate party—the Yugoslav Muslim People's Organization (JMNO), which won only one vote for every ten votes garnered by Spaho's JMO in the parliamentary elections of 18 March 1923.[11]

Without the pro-Serbian dissidents, the JMO was free to chart its course together with the other anticentralist parties that had legitimated themselves in the elections of 1923 as the authentic voices of their national communities and sought the revision of the Vidovdan constitution. As a result, the emerging federalist bloc of principal Croat, Slovene, and Bosnian Muslim parties— respectively, Stjepan Radić's Croat Republican Peasant Party (HRSS), Anton Korošeć's Slovene People's Party (SLS), and Spaho's JMO—took shape in 1923 as an expression of growing opposition to Serbian hegemony. For their part, the ruling Serbian Radicals responded by warning that any attempts at restoration of Bosnian autonomy would be resisted by the Serbs. Still, in their eagerness to stem the influence of the federalist bloc, the radicals first committed Radić's HRSS to continued parliamentary abstinence (April 1923), then disappointed federalist maneuvering with Davidović's Democrats by establishing a strict centralist government with Davidović's dissidents (March 1924), and finally resorted to obstructionist methods in order to postpone the loss of confidence in the parliament (May 1924).

In Radić's absence (he illegally crossed the frontier in July 1923 with the aim of persuading various European governments to come to the aid of the Yugoslav opposition), the JMO increasingly took the lead in shaping the antiradical coalitions. The oppositional bloc of Davidović's Democrats, JMO, SLS, several smaller parties, and supported by Radić's HRSS, coalesced in the spring of 1924, only to gain the unexpected royal nod to form the government in July 1924. This first Muslim experience of tangible power (with four cabinet posts allotted to the JMO, Spaho became the minister of finances and Halil Hrasnica the minister of justice) was preceded by growing anti-Muslim violence that was encouraged by local Radical party officials in Bosnia-Herzegovina and was accompanied by a vociferous harangue against "Turks in power." It was also short-lived.

King Aleksandar had no intention of maintaining Davidović's cabinet, which he increasingly saw as an obstacle to his prerogatives and a challenge to his stranglehold over the armed forces.

In October 1924 he exacted the cabinet's resignation and then proceeded to resurrect the earlier Pašić's cabinet, which was charged with carrying out special repressive measures against the HRSS in advance of the newly announced round of parliamentary elections, scheduled for February 1925. During this period the government extended the anticommunist laws to the HRSS, charging Radić with having made his party an affiliate of the Comintern before his return to Yugoslavia in August 1924, after an extended tour of foreign capitals that included Moscow. The leadership of the HRSS was arrested, Radić included, but the governmental attempts to frighten the opposition did not bypass the JMO, whose members were exposed to the terror of Serbian veterans (Chetniks) and the demands by Radical leaders for the "Serbianization of Muslims" (Purivatra, 1974, 273 n. 24).

The elections of February 1925 reestablished the hegemony of the JMO among the Bosnian Muslims but failed to resolve Yugoslavia's internal divisions. Pašić's new government, however, felt that the narrow majority that it enjoyed required new efforts at securing the compliance of the federalist opposition. It succeeded in pressuring the imprisoned Radić into renouncing his republicanism, thereby opening the door to his entirely unprecedented, albeit brief, participation in radical cabinets (1925–26). More important, it reestablished the principle of cohabitation with federalist/autonomist partners, who were often as abused as they were useful. Given the JMO's particularly difficult situation, the escalation of murderous attacks against the Muslims by the Serbs, especially in eastern Bosnia-Herzegovina in the mid-1920's (incidents in the villages of Šahovići, Bahori, Vilogorac), the growing realization that oppositional politics led to a dead end, and the example of Radić, it is easy to understand why Spaho welcomed with relief the invitation of Pašić's Radical successor Velja Vukićević to join the government in April 1927, where the JMO remained after the elections of September 1927, and the reconstruction of Vukićević's cabinet in February 1928 (Purivatra, 1974, 304–94). It is more surprising, however, that the JMO stood solidly with the radicals against the escalating Radić opposition and remained in the Vukićević and Korošec cabinets after the assassination of Stjepan Radić and his two colleagues by a radical deputy in the summer of 1928.

The unraveling of Yugoslav parliamentarianism was seen as an opportunity by King Aleksandar, who had long undermined the country's political system. On 6 January 1929 he proclaimed his personal regime, stating that henceforth no intermediaries will stand between himself and the people. The dictatorship of King Aleksandar was dedicated to Yugoslav unitarism, but in fact fostered Serbianization under the guise of unitarist zeal. All the "confessional or tribal" parties, including the JMO, were banned and dispersed, but the king was careful to pick various renegades of non-Serb parties for the dictatorial cabinet. These included Salih Baljić, a former JMO deputy who was previously considered a Muslim of Croat orientation. Dictatorial offices were opened wide to Spaho's opponents from the early 1920s (Hamdija Karamehmedović) and long-standing Muslim Serbophiles (Avdo Hasanbegović). Mufti Maglajlić became the *reis ul-ulema* (Purivatra, 1974, 429–32).

The most overt anti-Muslim measure of the Aleksandrine dictatorship was the dismantling of precarious Bosnia-Herzegovina, which could be imagined from the common outline of its six districts. The king's point man in this effort was Milan Srškić, the leader of Bosnia's Serb radicals, who had long criticized what he viewed as his party's attempts to "cuddle the Turks." Srškić felt that "Bosnia-Herzegovina, both as a regional individuality and as a geographical concept, must forever disappear" (Purivatra, 1974, 415). A bigot, who once confessed to "being pained by the sight of minarets in Bosnia" (Meštrović, 1961, 242), he had a hand in Aleksandar's partitioning of Bosnia-Herzegovina out of existence by way of establishing the nine new administrative units, or banates (3 October 1929), that replaced the thirty-three districts of 1922. Four of the new banates (Vrbas, Drina, Littoral, Zeta) included parts of Bosnia-Herzegovina, but always in combination with neighboring Croatian, Serbian, and Montenegrin districts, and, except with the littoral, designed to yield a Serb majority. The slight revisions in the borders of the banates that were effected on 28 August 1931 had as little effect on the dictatorship's hostility to the historical provinces as Aleksandar's pseudo-Constitution of 3 September 1931 had on stemming the autocratic royal regime.[12] The representatives of the banned parties voiced their opposition to the new order in a series of formal resolutions that were promulgated in the fall of 1931. The JMO's resolution called for the reconstruction of the country along "political-historical units with the broadest powers." Bosnia-Hercegovina had to be one of these units (Boban, 1962, 345–46).

The assassination of King Aleksandar in October 1934 and the establishment of the regency under Prince Pavle hastened the crisis of the royal dictatorship, which had floundered in pseudo-parliamentary guise since 1931. Most of the opposition, including Spaho's JMO, joined Radić's successor Vladko Maček, the president of the Croat Peasant Party (HSS), in forming the United Opposition to the government in the elections of May 1935 (Stojkov, 1969, 298–300). But although these rigged elections produced an electoral majority for the regency, Prince Pavle preferred to install a new prime minister, Milan Stojadinović, who proceeded to broaden the base of the governing bloc by enticing the JMO into the ruling coalition that included former radicals (among them, Stojadinović himself), Slovenes (SLS), and HSS renegades (Čulinović, 1961, vol. 2, 99–100). The new ruling party, the Yugoslav Radical Union (JRZ, or popularly Jereza, which sounded suspiciously like "heresy"), grew out of this governing combination in August 1935.

The opportunistic policy of the JMO protected the interests of the Muslims under Stojadinović's increasingly repressive regime but did not impose the issue of Bosnia-Herzegovina as a priority item for state reconstruction. Hence, when Prince Pavle decided to dispose of Stojadinović in February 1939 and pursue the course of negotiations with the Croat opposition, the results were disappointing for the Muslims. The Sporazum (Agreement) that the regent's new prime minister, Dragiša Cvetković, reached with Maček's HSS, sanctioned the establishment of autonomous Croatia (Banovina Hrvatska), which included parts of historical Bosnia-Herzegovina, specifically the communes of Derventa, Gradačac, and Brčko (south of the Sava), Travnik, Bugojno, Fojnica, Prozor, Tomislav Grad (Duvno), and Livno (central and southwestern Bosnia), and Konjic, Ljubuški, Mostar, and Stolac (western Herzegovina). The remaining thirty-eight communes of Bosnia-Herzegovina were reserved for the projected Serbian portion of Yugoslavia, thereby encouraging the Serbs to look on most of Bosnia-Herzegovina as legitimately Serbian. The division was effected by discounting the Muslims altogether. For example, if in a given commune the Catholics constituted 31 percent of the population and the Orthodox 30 percent, the commune went to Croatia. The Muslim plurality made no difference.

Maček, like Radić before him, sought to limit the hold of the JMO over the Bosnian Muslims. Mehmed Spaho, the chief target of this policy, died at the height of Maček's negotiations with Prime Minister Cvetković. Džafer-beg Kulenović, Spaho's successor, was a Muslim of pronounced Croat sentiment and an exponent of a pro-HRSS/HSS stand since 1921 (Purivatra, 1974, 154–55). But he was no less firm in having Bosnia-Herzegovina recognized as the Yugoslavia's "fourth unit," together with Slovenia, Croatia, and Serbia. Having failed in this effort, Kulenović and the JMO sought to portray autonomous Croatia as a temporary arrangement in its Bosnian part: "The definite borders of our country's administrative units will be established only in the new constitution, which will replace the current constitution and represent the final word in this matter" (Boban, 1965, 259). Kulenović's opposition to the division of Bosnia-Herzegovina between Serbia and Croatia[13] was seconded by most Muslims, whether of Croat or Serb orientation. For the Croat leadership, however, the agreement with the Serbs was a more important consideration than the hostile reaction of Bosnian Muslims. Serbs were more likely to accept a divided Bosnia than Bosnian autonomy (Jareb, 1960, 69).

During World War II, Bosnia-Herzegovina became an integral part of the collaborationist Independent State of Croatia (NDH). The Ustaša dictatorship provided no autonomy for Bosnia-Herzegovina, which was broken up among twelve provinces (grand *župas*), seven of which (Hum, Krbava-Psat, Lašva-Glaž, Pliva-Rama, Sana-Luka, Usora-Soli, Vrhbosna) had centers in former Bosnia-Herzegovina, and in the cases of the first two included three counties of former Croatia-Slavonia and Dalmatia. By contrast, five grand *župas* with centers outside Bosnia-Herzegovina (Dubrava, Gora, Livac-Zapolje, Posavje, Vuka) acquired thirteen Bosnian-Herzegovinian counties. Croatian integralism as practiced in Bosnia-Herzegovina was consistent with Ustaša ideology, whereby the Bosnian Muslims were simply Croats of Islamic confession. According to Ante Pavelić (1942, 2), the "Croat national consciousness never was extinguished in the Muslim element of Bosnia, and after the departure of the Turks has resurfaced."

Pavelić never failed to woo the Muslims with a show of respect for their religion, symbols, and decor. For example, he ordered that the circular Art Pavilion of Ivan Meštrović in Zagreb be augmented with three high minarets and turned into a mosque, which was pointedly named the Poglavnik's Mosque[14] (*Poglavnik* was Pavelić's title, meaning leader/ Führer).

But despite the presence of Ademaga Mešić, Džafer-beg Kulenović, Osman-beg Kulenović, Hakija Hadžić, and a few other
Muslim notables in his wider entourage, he never really shared
power with the Muslims, nor was such sharing seriously con-
templated by the real Ustaša arbiters of Bosnia-Herzegovina
(Andrija Artuković, Vjekoslav Luburić, Rafael Boban), who
were Croats of Catholic background. Typically, in the second—
and more considered—round of appointments in the fall of
1941, Pavelić named twenty Ustaša movement leaders (*stožer-
nici*) for the most of grand *župa*s. None of these men were
Muslims, including the seven appointed to the grand *župa*s with
centers in Bosnia-Herzegovina. Of the seven, all but one were
from Croat hubs in western Herzegovina and western Bosnia,
and one was from neighboring Dalmatia.[15]

Harsh repression against Serbs was Ustaša state policy and
was carried out systematically in Bosnia-Herzegovina. Massacres and terror provoked Serb flight into forested areas and the
beginnings of resistance. At first, this mass of desperate and
frightened villagers was not led by any organized political force,
and hence frequently was susceptible to demagogical calls for
revenge. For their part, the Ustašas sought to implicate the
Muslims in their anti-Serb violence. Muslim protests from 1941
speak of conscious "Catholic" attempts to blame the Muslims
for the Ustaša massacres and to explain these events as a "re-
ciprocal squaring of accounts between the Muslims and the
[Serb] Orthodox." To that end, the Muslims charged, Ustašas
masqueraded as Muslims, frequently wearing fezzes, "which
were introduced as [part of] the uniform for the whole army,
all along committing various crimes, in the course of which they
addressed one another by Muslim names" ("Sarajevska rezolucija," 1984, 510).

In the second half of 1941, members of the Muslim ulema
and other notables from several cities (Sarajevo, Prijedor, Mostar, Banja Luka, Bijeljina, Tuzla) wrote vociferous protests to

the German authorities denouncing any association with the Ustaša crimes. These protests speak to the fear of the Muslim elite that the Ustašas would succeed in poisoning Muslim relations with the Serbs.[16] But although the protest resolutions condemned a "handful of so-called Muslims," who participated in Ustaša repression ("Rezolucija muslimana," n.d., 512), they could not placate Serbian royalist Chetniks and their commanders in Bosnia (Jezdimir Dangić, Momčilo Djujić, Dobrosav Jevdjević), who were bent on turning recompense for persecution into an anti-Muslim campaign. From the summer of 1941, the Chetniks increasingly gained control over Serb insurgents and carried out gruesome crimes against Muslims of eastern Bosnia-Herzegovina. Massacres of Muslims, usually by cutting the throats of victims and tossing the bodies into various waterways, occurred especially in eastern Bosnia, in Foča, Goražde, Čajniče, Rogatica, Višegrad, Vlasenica, Srebrenica, all in the basin of the Drina, but also in eastern Herzegovina, where individual villages resisted Serb encirclement with ferocious determination until 1942.[17]

Chetnik documents—for example, the minutes of the Chetnik conference in Javorine, district of Kotor Varoš, in June 1942— speak of a determination to "cleanse Bosnia of everything that is not Serb" (Dedijer and Miletić, 1990, 166). It is difficult to estimate the number of Muslim victims of this original "ethnic cleansing," but it can be counted in the tens of thousands. Bosnian Muslims lost 86,000 people during the war, or 6.8 percent of their population (Kočović, 1985, 124), mainly to Chetnik terror. In the early months of insurgency, however, the then predominantly Serb Partisans, themselves initially in an uneasy alliance with the Chetniks, were susceptible to anti-Muslim repression. For example, the taking of Borač, a Muslim enclave in eastern Herzegovina, in April 1942, was accompanied by pillage, burning of houses, and slaughter of women and children. Moreover, the Communists were obliged to hide the nationality of their Muslim and Croat commanders from their predominantly Serb base (Vukmanović-Tempo, 1971, vol. 1, p. 195). Osman Karabegović, the political commissar of the Partisan operational staff for northwestern Bosnia, remembered how an old Serb woman gave him and another Partisan shelter in January 1942, at Manjasa: "As she covered us with woolen coverings, the old woman spoke: 'Rest, children, sleep peacefully. And may God save you from accursed Turks.' She could not expect that my name was Osman and my comrade's—Mujo" (Karabegović, 1978, 99).

Tito's Partisans in Bosnia-Herzegovina quickly shed Serb exclusivity and picked up the banner of Bosnian statehood as one of their auxiliary causes. Tito anticipated this position at the Fifth Land Conference of the Communist Party of Yugoslavia (KPJ), held underground in Zagreb (October 1940), when he noted that "Bosnia is one, because of centuries-old common life, regardless of confession" (Damjanović, Bosić, and Lazarević, 1980, 214). At the same time, he did not contradict Milovan Djilas's rejection of a notion that Bosnian Muslims were an "ethnic group" (that is, less than a nationality), which was proposed by a Muslim Communist (Mustafa Pašić). Indeed, the literature of the period did not attempt to define the Muslims in any specific "ethnic" sense but recognized them as a community with rights equal to that of Serbs and Croats.[18] Rodoljub Čolaković, a leading Serb Communist from Bosnia, noted in a parliamentary speech of January 1946 that the "Muslims of Bosnia-Herzegovina, as a separate—but, for the most part, still nationally undeclared—Slavic ethnic group, [were] equal to Serbs and Croats" (Purivatra, 1970, 122).

The notion that the Muslims must "declare" themselves as either Serbs or Croats pushed back the idea of their separate national identity in the period from the late 1940s to the early 1960s. This was the time of Serb predominance in Bosnia-Herzegovina, which coincided with the persecution of Islam, the trials of the Young Muslims from 1946 to 1949,[19] the imposition of a pliant ulema leadership (Sulejman Kemura) by the authorities, and the espousal of Serb nationhood by most high-level Bosnian Muslim cadres (Avdo Humo, Hajro Kapetanović, Šefket Maglajlić, Hakija Pozderac), with a minority opting for the "Yugoslav" category (Džemal Bijedić, Osman Karabegović, Pašaga Mandžić).[20] For all that, Muslims used the cult of Tito to legitimate Bosnian identity. In the stanza of Hamza Humo, "In our Bosnia the written signs stand / On the slabs of Bogomils;/—The road to Tito is clearly chiseled on the rock; . . . Comrades! / Bosnia finally found its way . . ." (Humo, 1976, vol. 1, p. 268).

After 1966, however, Tito increasingly relied on Bosnia-Herzegovina's hard-line Communist leadership, now evenly apportioned among the three communities, against deviationist trends in both Serbia and Croatia. He simultaneously promoted the Bosnian Muslims as a full-fledged *national* group, thereby propelling them into an increasingly favored position that came at the price of compliance. This was the period of Tito's favorite Džemal Bijedić, the prime minister of Yugoslavia from 1971 to his death in a plane crash in 1977, which has been portrayed as an assassination. More than any other single Communist leader of Muslim origin, Bijedić insisted on the affirmation of Bosnian Muslim nationhood, stressing that "from Turkish times until today it is incontrovertible that the Muslims showed their national steadfastness and persistence" (Bartolović, 1985, 135).

Orthodox Titoism of the superfederalist period had a strong base among the Muslims of Bosnia-Herzegovina, who emerged as the dominant community in their republic, to the great chagrin of Bosnian Serbs. Nevertheless, although Islam underwent a renaissance in Bosnia-Herzegovina in the 1970s and 1980s, it cannot be said that the official authorization of mosque building and the toleration of public piety and pilgrimage lessened the secular character of Bosnia-Herzegovina. This is obvious from the art of the period, notably the poems of Mak Dizdar, the novels of Meša Selimović, and the paintings of Mersad Berber. The pecularities of Bosnian Muslim socialist nationhood, whereby one can be a Muslim by nationality and a Jehovah's Witness by religion (this is not a bizarre invention but a commonplace in the town of Zavidovići) became fully accepted in the Bosnian Muslim community. Ever since Tito's death in 1981, Serbian appetites in Bosnia have been on the rise. The "Memorandum of the Serbian Academy of Sciences and Arts" (1986), which is usually regarded as the intellectual justification of and the prodromus to contemporary Serbian nationalism, included a denunciation of "artificially established, new, regional literatures," among them the literature of Bosnia-Herzegovina: "Practically until yesterday Meša Selimović was not permitted to identify himself as a Serb writer, his insistence on belonging to Serb literature not being respected even now. . . . In this way the Serb culture and spiritual heritage emerges as less significant than it is, thereby depriving the Serb people of an important footing for their moral and historical self-consciousness" ("Memorandum SANU," 1989, 44).

The case against the Agrokomerc conglomerate of Velika Kladuša in 1987 was the first shot in the campaign against the Muslim party bosses in Bosnia-Herzegovina, aimed straight at Hamdija Pozderac, the vice president of Yugoslavia, whose turn at the chair of the rotating Yugoslav presidency would have commenced in May 1988, was one of Slobodan Milošević's first intrigues against the Muslim leadership.[21] After the collapse of the party center in January 1990, Bosnia-Herzegovina, too, followed the path of political pluralism. The new parties, all organized along national lines, easily won against the reformed Communists in November 1990. The new coalition was not easily shaped, but it included the (Muslim) Party of Democratic Action, headed by Alija Izetbegović, whom the Bosnian parliament then elected as the president of Bosnia-Herzegovina.

This is not the proper place for an analysis of everything that happened in Bosnia since that time, especially after Bosnia's independence in the spring of 1992. Nevertheless, since President Izetbegović frequently is accused of "Islamic fundamentalism" by the Serbian leadership (and most recently by the Croat leadership, as well), it would be useful to note that none of his actions have given credence to these charges. Izetbegović consistently has championed a secular, multinational Bosnian state, in which the rights of the three constituent communities would be guaranteed and protected. The new flag of Bosnia is a throwback, not to the Renaissance-invented Ottoman scimitar that was adopted by the Habsburgs after 1878, but to the nondescript Kotromanić fleurs-de-lis of the medieval period. Nor is there any basis for suspicions about Izetbegović that can be deduced from his position paper usually referred to as the "Islamic Declaration" (written in 1969–70), for which he was tried and sentenced to an exceedingly harsh term of fourteen years of penal servitude in 1983.

The declaration is really an espousal of reconciliation between Islamic religious tradition and progress. It argues that the benefits of Western civilization cannot be acquired on their own terms, without spiritual support that is inherent in the tradition of non-Western societies ("The Islamic Declaration," 1983, 61):

> There are reforms which reflect the wisdom of a nation and there are those that betoken its own betrayal. Japan and Turkey are classic examples of this in contemporary history. At the turn of the century, these two countries offered a picture of very similar, hence "comparable" countries. . . . Then followed the well known reforms in both countries. In order to live its own, and not an alien life, Japan attempted to combine tradition and progress. The Turkish modernists, however, chose the contrary path. Today, Turkey is a third-rate country whereas Japan has climbed to the very summit of the world's nations. . . . [Japan] kept her own complicated script which, after reforms, contains 880 Chinese

ideograms in addition to 46 symbols. Today, there is no illiteracy in Japan whereas in Turkey, forty years after the introduction of the Latin script, more than half the population is illiterate, a consequence which even a blind man could have foreseen. . . . Turkey lost its "memory," its past. . . . As a consequence of this vandalism in Turkey and elsewhere, "counterfeit nations" have been created or are on the way to being created: spiritually confused countries without their own physiognomies and sense of direction.

In the declaration, Izetbegović speaks against the wide gulf between the intelligentsia and the masses in Muslim countries. Although he champions a new Islamic order, he underscores its commitment to the freedom of conscience, women's rights, and so forth. There is no reference to Bosnia-Herzegovina in the declaration. Moreover, Izetbegović notes ("The Islamic Declaration," 1983, 76) that the

Islamic order can be realized only in those countries in which Moslems represent the majority of the population. Without this majority, the Islamic system is reduced only to naked power (because the second element, the Islamic society, is missing) and may turn into tyranny. Non-Moslem minorities within an Islamic state, on condition of loyalty, enjoy religious freedom and every protection. Moslem minorities within non-Islamic communities, conditional on a guarantee of religious freedom and a normal life and development, are loyal and duty bound to observe every obligation to that community with the exception of those harming Islam and Moslems.

His main thought is that the Koran permits modernization but also that modernization in the Islamic world can succeed only if it is rooted in Islam.

The desperate situation of the Bosnian Muslims, whose country is currently being destroyed while the world ignores the agony of Sarajevo, Goražde, Srebrenica, Mostar, and so many lesser places, has not significantly eroded the progressive bloc of Bosnian Islam. There is a grave danger, however, that abandonment by the West, and in South Slavic affairs by Croatia, can lead to a drastic sea-change in Bosnian Muslim allegiances. It is difficult to imagine how the disappearance of Bosnia-Herzegovina, that is, the permanent statelessness of Bosnian Muslims, can possibly contribute to Balkan stability. The European West can come to terms with European Muslims, but only when communication ceases to be based on the model of the conversation between Nasruddin Hoca and the Frenchman.

NOTES

1. The literature on the Church of Bosnia, is voluminous and frequently contradictory. For the most authoritative up-to-date collection on the various aspects of this subject, see Šidak (1975).
2. On the history of the Franciscan order in Bosnia, see esp. Jelenić (1912–15). See also a recent collection-catalogue by Sorić (1988).
3. On the history of Eastern Orthodoxy in Bosnia-Herzegovina, Slijepčević, (1966, vol. 2, 497–561).
4. On the migrations that were prompted by the Ottoman conquest, see Djurdjev, Grafenauer, and Tadić (1959, vol. 2, 840–53).
5. On the conversions of Bosnian Catholics to Eastern Orthodoxy, see St. Draganović (1937).
6. On the course of Bosnian history under the Ottomans, see Djurdjev (1959, 114–58, 477–512, 582–612, 1318–41).
7. For a brief history of Bosnian Islam, see Hadžijahić, Traljić, and Šukrić (1977).
8. On the Habsburg period of Bosnian history, see esp. Imamović (1976). For a discussion of the Muslim movement for religious autonomy under the Habsburg regime, see Šehić (1980).
9. On the history of the Catholic church in Bosnia-Herzegovina under the Habsburgs, see Djuro Kokša, "Uspostava redovite hijerarhije, u BiH 1881," in Petar Babić and Mato Zovkić, eds., *Katolička crkva u Bosni i Hercegovini u XIX i XX stoljeću* (Sarajevo, 1986), pp. 21–60.
10. On the position of Bosnian Muslims in the early years of royalist Yugoslavia, see Banac (1984, 359–77).

11. On the split within the JMO, see Purivatra, *Jugoslavenska mus-limanska*, pp. 141–59.

12. On the borders of Aleksandar's "watery" banates, see Boban (1992, 29–37).

13. At the end of January 1944, Kulenović stated that he would "most of all like that the whole people of Bosnia-Herzegovina be asked to decide by vote whether they prefer the autonomy of Bosnia-Herzegovina or its division and accession of one part to Croatia and the other to Serbia. I am certain that the people in Bosnia-Herzegovina would favor my position by absolute majority"; cited in Boban (1974, vol. 2, p. 233).

14. On the history of this unusual edifice, see Blaskovich (1992).

15. Reconstructed from the information in Jelić-Butić (1977, 111). Krizman (1978, 564–74).

16. For more on these resolutions, see Jelić-Butić (1977, 201–2).

17. On the Chetnik massacres of Muslims in Bosnia-Herzegovina, see Dedijer and Miletić (1990).

18. This is exactly how Tito addressed the Muslim issue. His important article, "The National Question in Yugoslavia in the Light of the National-Liberation Struggle" (December 1942), includes the following passages: "The term 'national-liberation struggle' would be only a phrase, moreover deception, if it did not have—in addition to its general Yugoslav sense—a national sense for each separate people, that is, if—in addition to the liberation of Yugoslavia—it did not also mean the liberation of the Croats, Slovenes, Serbs, Macedonians, Albanians, Muslims, etc." Josip Broz Tito, "Nacionalno pitanje u Jugoslaviji u svetlosti narodno-oslobodilačke borbe," *Proleter* (Drinići) 17, no. 16 (1942), 3. Note that Tito used the term *muslimani* (in lower case) for the Muslims, thereby signaling their non-national status.

19. On these trials, which ended with very harsh sentences for some two hundred defendants, administrative punishment for others, and four executions (Hasan Biber, Nusref Fazlibegović, Halid Kajtaz, Omer Stupac), see Trjulj (1992). One of the defendants in these trials was Alija Izetbegović, the future president of Bosnia-Herzegovina, then twenty-one years old.

20. Information based on Marković (1957).
21. For more on this complex case, see Šošić (1989).

REFERENCES

Banac, Ivo. (1984). *The National Question in Yugoslavia: Origins, History, Politics.* Ithaca, N.Y.

Bartolović, Dragan. (1985). *Dzemal Bijedić i njegovo vrijeme.* Mostar.

Blaskovich, Jerry Nick. (1992). "The Zagreb Mosques: A Study of Non-Muslim Sponsorship of Islamic Art in the Balkan Heart of Cristendom." M.A. thesis, University of California, Los Angeles.

Boban, Ljubo. (1962). "Zagrebačke punktacije." *Istorija XX veka* (Belgrade), 4, 345–46.

———. (1965). *Sporazum Cvetković-Maček.* Belgrade.

Boban, Ljubo. (1992). *Hrvatske granice, 1918–1992.* Zagreb.

Boban, Ljubo. (1974). *Maček i politika Hrvatske seljačke stranke, 1928–1941* (2 vols.) Zagreb.

Čulinović, Ferdo. (1961). *Jugoslavija izmedju dva rata* (2 vols.). Zagreb.

Damjanović, Pero, Milovan Bosić, and Dragica Lazarević (Eds.). (1980). *Peta zemaljska konferencija KPJ (19–23, oktobar 1940).* Belgrade.

Dedijer, Vladimir, and Antun Miletić (Eds.). (1990). *Genocid na Muslimanima, 1941–1945: Zbornik dokumenata i svedočenja.* Sarajevo.

Djurdjev, Branislav, Bogo Grafenauer, and Jorjo Tadić (Eds.). (1959). *Historija naroda Jugoslavije* (2 vols). Zagreb.

Frndić, Nasko (Ed.). (1972). "Nasrudin-hodza i Francuz." In *Narodni humor i mudrost Muslimana.* Zagreb.

Hadžijahić, Muhamed. (1974). *Od tradicije do identiteta (Geneza nacionalnog pitanja bosanskih Muslimana).* Sarajevo.

Hadžijahić, Muhamed, Mahmud Traljić, and Nijaz Šukrić. (1977). *Islam i muslimani u Bosni i Hercegovini.* Sarajevo.

Humo, Hamza. (1976). "Zapisi na stečku." *Sabrana djela* (2 vols.). Sarajevo.

Imamović, Mustafa, (1976). *Pravni položaj i unutrašnji politički razvitak Bosne i Hercegovine 1878–1914.* Sarajevo.

"The Islamic Declaration: A Programme for the Islamicisation of Moslems and Moslem Peoples." (1983). *South Slav Journal* (London), 6(1), 61.

Jareb, Jere. (1960). *Pola stoljeća hrvatske politike*. Buenos Aires.

Jelenić, Julijan. (1912–15). *Kultura i bosanski franjevci* (2 vols.). Sarajevo.

Jelić-Butić, Fikreta. (1977). *Ustaše i Nezavisna država Hrvatska 1941–1945*. Zagreb.

Karabegović, Osman. (1978). *Krajina na putevima revolucije*. Belgrade.

Kočović, Bogoljub. (1985). *Žrtve Drugog svetskog rata u Jugoslaviji*. London.

Kokša, Djuro. (1986). "Uspostava redovite hijerarhije u BiH 1881." In Petar Babić and Mato Zovkić (Eds.), *Katolička crkva u Bosni i Hercegovini u XIX u XX stoljecu* (21–60). Sarajevo.

Kraljačić, Tomislav. (1987). *Kalajev režim u Bosni i Hercegovini (1882–1903)*. Sarajevo.

Krizman, Bogdan. (1978). *Pavelić i ustaše*. Zagreb.

Marković, Draza, et al. (Eds.). (1957). *Ko je ko u Jugoslaviji: Biografski podaci o jugoslovenskim savremenicima*. Belgrade.

"Memorandum SANU." (1989). *Duga* (Belgrade). (June), 44.

Meštrović, Ivan. (1961). *Uspomene na političke ljude i dogadjaje*. Buenos Aires.

Pavelić, Ante. (1942). "Pojam Bosne kroz stoljeća." *Spremnost Zagreb) (1 March)*, 2.

Purivatra, Atif. (1970). *Nacionalni i politički razvitak Muslimana*. Sarajevo.

———. (1974). *Jugoslavenska muslimanska organizacija u političkom životu Kraljevine Srba, Hrvata i Slovenaca*. Sarajevo.

"Rezolucija muslimana grada Mostara 1941. godine." *Bosanski pogledi: Nezavisni list muslimana Bosne i Hercegovine u iseljeništvu; pretisak*. London.

St. Draganović, K. (1937). *Massenübertritte von Katholiken zur "Orthodoxie" im kroatischen Sprachgebiet zur Zeit der Türkenherrschaft*. Rome.

Salihagić, Suljaga. (1940). *Mi bos. herc. muslimani u krilu jugoslovenske zajednice.* Banja Luka.

"Sarajevska rezolucija od oktobra 1941." (1984). *Bosanski pogledi: Nezavisni list muslimana Bosne i Hercegovine u iseljeništvu; pretisak.* London.

Šehić, Nusret. (1980). *Autonomni pokret Muslimana za vrijeme austrougarske uprave u Bosni i Hercegovini.* Sarajevo.

Šidak, Jaroslav. (1975). *Studije o "Crkvi bosanskoj" i bogumilstvu.* Zagreb.

Slijepčević, Djoko. (1966). *Istorija Srpske pravoslavne crkve* (2 vols.). Munich.

Sorić, Ante (Ed.). (1988). *Franjevci Bosne i Hercegovine na raskršću kultura i civilizacija.* Zagreb.

Šosić, Hrvoje. (1989). *Treće pokriće "Agrokomerca."* Zagreb.

Stojkov, Todor. (1969). *Opozicija u vreme šestojanuarske diktature, 1929–1935.* Belgrade.

Tito, Josip Broz. (1942). "Nacionalno pitanje u Jugoslaviji u svetlosti narodno-oslobodilačke borbe" (The National Question in Yugoslavia in the Light of the National-Liberation Struggle). *Proleter* 17(16) (December), 3.

Trhulj, Sead. (1992). *Mladi Muslimani.* Zagreb.

Vukmanović-Tempo, Svetozar. (1971). *Revolucija koja teče: Memoari.* (2 vols.). Belgrade.

Information Resources and Maps

In keeping with the goal of enhancing the reader's understanding of the area and mindful of the fact that this is the information age, a brief explanation of how these resource lists were generated will help interested readers expand or update them in the future. For the convenience of the general reader, little foreign language material was included in this section, although many of the works listed include references to foreign language material. The bibliographies in book form on Eastern Europe, the Balkans, or Yugoslavia were one-time publications. However, each of them contained some listings of ongoing sources, such as journals or series of publications. In addition to the listings of journals in those bibliographies, the *Academic Writer's Guide* (a work unfortunately never updated) can be used to identify journals that either deal with the area across a range of disciplines or deal with one discipline and frequently have coverage of Eastern Europe or the Balkans. The annual bibliographies published by the American Association for the Advancement of Slavic Studies and its European counterpart contain subdivisions for different countries and regions and different disciplines, and although they lag somewhat behind the chronological year, they are among the best guides to articles published in various journals or conference proceedings and to various kinds of nonbook materials.

The works listed were included because I know them. Readers who may want to expand this list to include future works can do so by simply calling some of the listed items up on the computerized catalog of any large library, noting the subject headings used for the earlier works, and then running a new search on those subject headings.

The individual items were downloaded from the Harvard University catalog, providing a somewhat standardized format for the newer items. In a few cases, where the simple author and title information is not enough to explain the work or its relevance here, some other parts of the record have been included.

The listing of maps was compiled from two sources. The first section includes mainly older maps held by Harvard libraries for which there was no machine-readable listing, only brief entries on cards. These cards were photocopied and then scanned into the computer with an optical scanner to allow for editing. The resulting list is a new resource. The second section (consisting mostly of newer maps) was created by searches on the words *Bosnia, Herzegovina,* and *Sarajevo* run in the MAPS file of the RLIN catalog, a multimillion-record catalog including the holdings of many libraries across the country. The results were downloaded, and those parts of the record of interest mainly to librarians were deleted. To update this list in future, the interested reader can have this search repeated.

To complete the listing of resources useful for keeping track of developments in Bosnia there remains a large range of electronic resources. To explain in even the briefest fashion the nature of the different kinds of resources and the differing means and terms of access I have found to be a tight squeeze even in a workshop of several hours. To compress this into a paragraph or two here would be impossible. Accordingly, here I list some of the kinds of resources available: (1) databases in various media (CD-ROM, online, offline etc.), (2) databases with differing terms of access (for a fee, free for those with access to Internet, direct free dial-ups), (3) databases with different types of structure (bibliographic, full-text, statistical databases), and (4) electronic resources other than databases (such as electronic newsletters, bulletin boards, conferences).

I. SOURCES FOR ADDITIONAL OR FUTURE INFORMATION ON BOSNIA

What follows is a brief bibliography for those who want either to delve deeper into the history of this area or follow the subject in the future. The focus here has been mainly on works in English or listing works in English to accommodate most readers. Those who do read various European languages can also use these to identify foreign language materials. The one-time publications afford not only material on the past but also list ongoing publications—journals or series in publication. The two annual bibliographies are generally a year or two behind the calendar year, but they cover all countries of the area in a wide range of disciplines.

Since many readers will find that their local libraries do not have some of these works, the International Standard Book (or Serial) Number (ISBN/ISSN) has been given to facilitate interlibrary locating and borrowing in today's world of computerized catalogs. Books printed before this system came into general use in the 1970s must still be searched the old way.

A. Bibliographies

1. *Eastern Europe as a Whole*

ANNUAL BIBLIOGRAPHIES

American Bibliography of Slavic and East European Studies. (1956–). Columbus, Ohio: American Association for the Advancement of Slavic Studies. ISSN: 0094-3770

European Bibliography of Soviet, East European and Slavonic Studies. Bibliographie européenne des travaux sur l'URSS et l'Europe de l'est. Europaische Bibliographie der Sowjet- und Osteuropastudien. T. Hnik (Ed., English, French, and German). (1975–). Birmingham: University of Birmingham. Vols. for 1975– sponsored by the International Committee for Soviet and East European Studies, with other institutions. ISSN 0140-492X.

ONE-TIME BIBLIOGRAPHIES

Bamborschke, Ulrich. (1981). *Bibliographie slavistischer Arbeiten aus den wichtigsten englischsprachigen Fachzeitschriften sowie Fest- und Sammelschriften 1992–1976 (Bibliography of Slavonic studies selected from the most important periodicals and miscellanies published in the English-speaking world 1922–76).* Bibliographische Mitteilungen des Osteuropa-Instituts an der Freien Universitat Berlin; Heft 19. Berlin: Osteuropa-Institut on der Freien Universitat Berlin; Wiesbaden: In Kommission bei O. Harrassowitz. ISBN 3447021829
Includes preface in English.

Carleton University, Institute of Soviet and East European Studies. ([1983]–1986). Bibliography. Nos. 1–5. Ottowa.

———. (1988). *Bibliographical series.* Russian series. 6. Gulf Breeze, Fla.: Academic International Press.

Communist Eastern Europe: Analytical Survey of Literature. (1971). Washington, D.C.: Department of the Army, DA Pam 550-8.

Horak, Stephan M. (1978). *Russia, the USSR, and Eastern Europe: A Bibliographic Guide to English Language Publications, 1964–1974.* Littleton, Colo.: Libraries Unlimited. ISBN 0872871789

Horak, Stephan M. (1982). *Russia, the USSR, and Eastern Europe: A*

Bibliographic Guide to English Language Publications, 1975–1980. Littleton, Colo.: Libraries Unlimited. ISBN 0872872971

Horak, Stephan M. (1987). *Russia, the USSR, and Eastern Europe: A Bibliographic Guide to English Language Publications, 1981–1985.* Littleton, Colo.: Libraries Unlimited. ISBN 087287561X

These three items by Horak continue the set mentioned in the Horecky entry below; the three areas that had a volume each in the 1960s set are here covered in each volume.

Russia and Eastern Europe, 1789–1985: A Bibliographical Guide. History and Related Disciplines, Select Bibliographies. (1989). Manchester: Manchester University Press. Distributed in the USA and Canada by St. Martin's Press. ISBN 0719017343

University of London, School of Slavonic and East European Studies. (1977–   ). *Bibliographical guides.* No. 1–   . London.

Slavic Studies: A Guide to Bibliographies, Encyclopedias, and Handbooks. (1993). Wilmington: Scholarly Resources. ISBN 0842023747

2. Bibliography on the Balkans

Horecky, Paul Louis. (1969). *Southeastern Europe: A Guide to Basic Publications.* Chicago.

Part of three-volume set covering the former USSR, East Central Europe, and Southeastern Europe.

3. Bibliographies on Certain Aspects of Eastern Europe

Birkos, Alexander S. (1975). *East European and Soviet Economic Affairs: A Bibliography (1965–1973).* Littleton, Colo.: Libraries Unlimited. ISBN 0872870979

Remington, Robin Alison. (1978). *The International Relations of Eastern Europe: A Guide to Information Sources.* International Relations Information Guide Series, vol. 8. Detroit: Gale Research Co. ISBN 0810313200

4. Listings of Periodicals on Eastern Europe

Academic Writer's Guide to Periodicals, Vol. 2, East European and Slavic Studies. (1971). Kent, Ohio: Kent State University Press.

Library of Congress, Slavic and Central European Division. (1967). *The USSR and Eastern Europe: Periodicals in Western Languages*

(3d ed.). Washington, D.C. Library of Congress; for sale by the Superintendant of Documents, U.S. Government Printing Office.

5. Bibliographies on Yugoslavia

Friedman. Francine. (in press). *Yugoslavia: A Comprehensive English-Language Bibliography*. Wilmington, Del.: Scholarly Resources. ISBN 0842023402

Horton, John Joseph. (1977). *Yugoslavia*. World bibliographical series. Oxford, Eng.: Clio Press; Santa Barbara, Calif.: American Bibliographical Center, Clio Press. ISBN 0903450097

Leskovsek, Valentin. (1974–82). *Yugoslavia: A Bibliography*. Vols. 9, 12–14. New York: Studia Slovenica.

Mihailovich, Vasa D. (1984). *A Comprehensive Bibliography of Yugoslav Literature in English, 1593–1980*. Columbus, Ohio: Slavica Publishers. ISBN 0893571369

Petrovich, Michael B. (1974). *Yugoslavia: A Bibliographic Guide*. Washington, D.C.: Slavic and Central European Division, Library of Congress.

B. Other Reference Works

1. Country Handbooks of the U.S. Government: Yugoslavia [updated irregularly]

Yugoslavia: A Country Study (2d ed.). (1982). Area handbook series, DA pam, 550–99. Washington, D.C.: Federal Research Division, Library of Congress; for sale by the Superintendant of Documents, U.S. Government Printing Office.

Yugoslavia; A Country Study (3d ed.). (1992). Area handbook series, DA pam, 550–99. Washington, D.C.: Federal Research Division, Library of Congress; for sale by the Superintendant of Documents, U.S. Government Printing Office.

2. Miscellaneous

Sudostinstitut. *Wissenschaftlicher Dienst Sudosteuropa*. Muenchen.

II. MAPS OF BOSNIA, HERZEGOVINA, OR SARAJEVO

A. In the Harvard Library Map Collection

This listing is by chronological order of the date of the map, which in several cases is earlier than that of the book containing it. Information in brackets was supplied by the cataloguer from sources other than the map, and a question mark indicates the cataloguer's estimate of the date.

1. [Zsamboki, Janos, 1531–1584]. Illyricum. [Antwerp, A. Ortelius, 1584] "Ioan. Sambucus Ortelio suo, s. mitto hanc quoque tabellam . . . Viennae . . . 1572." "Cum imperatiorie & regie maiestatis privilegio." Text in Latin on reverse side of sheet. A copy of a map found in [Ortelius, Abraham] *Theatrum orbis terrarum. Opus nunc tertio ab ipso auctore recognitum multisque locis castigatum et quamplurimis novis tabulis atque commentarijs auctum.* [Antwerp, A. Ortelius, 1584] Map no. 80.

2. [Hirschvogel Augustin, 1503–1553] Schlavoniae, Croatiae, Carniae, Istriae, Bosniae finitimarumque regionum nova descriptio, auctore Augustino Hirsvogelio. [Antwerp, A. Ortelius, 1584] "Cum privilegio." Text in Latin on reverse side of sheet. A copy of a map found in [Ortelius, Abraham] *Theatrum orbis terrarum. Opus nunc tertio ab ipso auctore recognitum multisque locis castigatum et quamplurimis novis tabulis atque commentarius auctum.* [Antwerp, A. Ortelius, 1584] Map no. 81.

3. [Mercator, Gerhard] Sclavonia Croatia, Bosnia, cum Dalmatiae parte. [Amsterdam, J. Janssonius, 163–?] A copy of a map found in *Nieuwen atlas ofte werelt-beschrijvinge vertoonende de voornaemste rijckenende landen des gheheelen aerdt-bodems; vermeerdert met veele schoone landt-kaerten, nieuwelijcks uptgegeven* . . . . Amsterdam, Ioannem Ianssonlum, 1657–[87]. 6 vols. Vol. 1, map no. 138.

4. Iadera, Sicum et Aenona, vulgo Zara, Sibenico et Nona, cum insulis adjacentibus in parte Dalmatiae boreali. Amsterdam, Ioannem Ianssonium, [1650?]. A copy of a map found in *Nieuwen atlas ofte werelt-beschrijvinge vertoonende de voornaemste rijckenende landen des gheheelen aerdt-bodems; vermeerdert met veele schoone landt-kaerten, nieuwelijcks uptgegeven* . . . Amsterdam, Ioannem Ianssonium, 1657–[87]. 6 vols. Vol. 5, map no. 32.

5. Illyricum hodiernum quod scriptores communiter Sclavoniam, Itali Schiavoniam nuncupare solent, in Dalmatiam, Croatiam, Bosnam et Slavoniam distinguitur . . . [Amsterdam], Ioannes Blaeu, [1663.] A copy of a map found in *Le grand atlas ou cosmographie Blaviane en laquelle est exactement descritte la terre, la mer et le ciel.* Amsterdam, Jean Blaeu, 1663. 12 vols. Vol. 2, map no. 33.

6. [Mercator, Gerhard] Sclavonia, Croatia, Bosnia, cum Dalmatiae parte. [Amsterdam, Janssonius-Waesbergios; Oxford, Moses Pitt, 1683?] "Per Gerardum Mercatorem, cum privilegio." A copy of map found in *The English Atlas* . . . Oxford, for Moses Pitt, 1680–83. 4 vols. Vol. 3, map no. 18.

7. Coronelli, [Vincenzo Maria] Le royaume de Dalmacie, divise en ses comtez territoires etc., la Morlaquie et la Bosnie. Paris, J. B. Nolin, [170–?] A copy of a map found in Fer, Nicolas de, *Atlas ou recueil de cartes geographiques, dressees sur les nouvelles observations de mrs. de l'Academie Royale des Sciences* . . . Paris, Desbois, 1746–[53]. Map no. 88.

8. [Valck, Gerhard, and Valck, Leonhard] Dalmatia, Sclavonia, Croatia, Bosnia, Servia et Istria, distributa in singulares ditiones et dioeceses, una cum republica Ragusana et circumjacentibus regionibus, Hungaria, Venetiis, Statu ecclesiastico, Neapoli et Macedonia. [Amsterdam], Gerardum et Leonardum Valk, [171–?].

9. Sclavonia, Croatia, Bosnia cum Dalmatiae parte. Amsterdam, P. Mortier, [171–?]. Dedication to dno. Petro comiti perpetuo de Zrin by Joannes Blaeu. Additional title: Illyricum hodiernum quod scriptores communiter Sclavoniam, Itali Schiavoniam nuncupare solent.

10. Neu geographisch vorgestelltes Ungarisches-kriegs-theatrum in Servien und dem Banat Temeswar, worinnen die glueckliche pro-

gressen kayserl. siegreichesten waffen unter commando des durchl. princ. Eugenii von Savojen mit allen bisher in zweyen feldzuegen 1716 und 1717 gehaltenen schlachten und eroberten platzen, in kupfer gewiesen werden. Nuernberg, Ioh. Bapt. Homann, [1717].

11. [Seutter, Georg Matthaeus]. Nova et accurata regnorum et provinciarum Dalmatiae, Croatiae, Sclavoniae, Bosniae, Serviae, Istriae et reip. Ragusanae cum finitimis regionibus. Augsburg, Matthaei Seutteri, [173–?]. A copy of a map found in *Atlas novus sive tabulae geographicae totius orbis faciem, partes, imperia, regna et provincias exhibentes, exactissima cura iuxta recentissimas observation.* Augsburg, Matthaeo Seutter, [1745?] 2 vols. Vol. 1, map no. 107.

12. [Coronelli, Vincenzo Maria]. le gouvernement de Raguse, estant une partie de Dalmatie, avec quelques isles tres exactement mis en escrit par le pere Corneille. [Amsterdam], Petrum Schenk Jun., [173?].

13. [Oettinger, Johann Friedrich von]. Theatrum belli inter imperat. Carol. VI et sult. Achmet IV in partibus regnorun Serviae et Bosniae ex authenticis subsidis delineatun a Ioh. Fr. Ottingero, loc. ten imper. Nuernberg. Homannianis Heredibus [1738]. "Cum p.s.c.m.gr." [Edition with imperial privilege].

14. Le royaume de Bosnie dans son entier; dedie a son excellence monseigr. le feld marechal comte de Khewenhueller . . . Vienna, Etienne Briffaut, [1740?].

15. Delisle, G[uillaume], and others. Nouvelle carte du royaume de Dalmacie divise en ses comtes, territoires etc., la Morlaquie, la Bosnie et la Servie, partie de la Hongrie, Croatie, Albanie, Istrie & du roy.e de Naples; par G. de L'Isle, Coronelli, G. I. Rossi et I. Nolin. Amsterdam, R. et I. Ottens, [174–?]. A copy of a map found in *Altas minor sive geographia compendiosa in qua orbis terrarum paucis attamen novissimis tabulis ostenditur. Atlas nouveau contenant toutes les parties du monde, ou sont exactement remarques les empires, monarchies, royaumes, etats, republiques &c.&c.&c.; receuillies des meilleurs auteurs.* Amsterdam, R. & J. Ottens, [1745?]. Map no. 94.

16. Tabula geographica exhibens regnum Sclavoniae cum Syrmii du-

catu; ex mappa grandiori desumta et in lucem edita. [Nuernberg], Hommanianis Heredibus, 1745. "C.p.s.c.m.gr." [Edition with imperial privilege].

17. Santini, [Francesco]. Nouvelle carte de la partie orientale de Dalmatie dressee sur les lieux. Venice, mr. Remondini], 1780. A copy of a map found in Santini, [Francesco], *Atlas universel dresse sur les meilleures cartes modernes.* Venice, Remondini, 1776–[84.] Vol. 2, map no. 17.

18. Santini, [Francesco]. Nouvelle carte de la partie occidentale de Dalmatie dressee sur les lieux. Venice, mr. Remondini], 1780. A copy of a map found in Santini, [Francesco], *Atlas universel dresse sur les meilleures cartes modernes.* Venice, Remondini, 1776–[84]. Vol. 2, map no. 18.

19. Reider, C. Continuatio mappae litho hydrographicae nationis Slavicae ad occidentem solem sitae. n.p., n. publ., 1787.

20. Schuetz, Carl. Neueste karte der koenigreiche Bosnien, Servien, Croatien und Slavonien samt den angraenzenden provinzen Temeswar, Dalmatien, Herzegowina, Ragusa, Steyermark, Kaernthen, Krain, Friaul, Gradiska und Istrien, einem grosen theil von Ungarn, Siebenbuergen, Walachei, Bulgarien, Albanien, Macedonien und einem stueck des kirchenstaats und k.reichs Neapel; nach den besten orginalzeichnungen charten und beschreibungen entworfen. Vienna, Artaria Compagnie, 1788.

21. [Schimeck, Maximilian]. Das koenigreich Bosnien und die Herzegovina (rama) samt den angraenzenden provinzen von Croatien, Sclavonien, Temesvar, Servien, Albanien, Ragusa und dem Venetianischen Dalmatien; nach den militaerischen handkarten des prinzen Eugen, der grafen Khevenhueller, Marsigli und Pallavicini geographisch aufgetragen und nach den zuverlaessigsten nachrichten und reisebeschreibungen berichtiget. Vienna, F. A. Schraembl, 1788. A copy of a map found in Schraembl, Franz Anton, *Allgeimeiner grosser atlass* . . . Vienna, P. J. Schalbacher, 1800. Map no. 28.

22. Neue kriegs-karte welche die graenzen zwischen den Oesterreichischen und Tuerkischen laendern Ungarn, Siebenbuergen und

Wallachey, dann Tuerkisch Croatien, Bosnien, Servien bis Widden in der Tuerkey enthaelt. n.p., n. publ., [1790?].

23. Karte von dem koenigreich Servien. Vienna, Artaria compagnie, [1790?].

24. Guessefeld, F[ranz] L[udwig]. Charte von Dalmatien nebst den angrenzenden Ungrischen, Osmanschen u. andern laendern. Nuernberg, Homann. Erben, 1798. Engraved by I. Rausch.

25. Die buchten von Cattaro und die republik Ragusa. Weimar, verlage des geograph. instituts, 1806.

26. Capellaris, Gioanni Antonio de. Carta novissima della Dalmazia, Albania, Croazia, Bosnia, con le provincie confinanti del Cragno, Schiavonia, Goriziano, Veneziano, Raguseo, Papalino e Napolitano. Vienna, Contojo delle Arte e dell'Industria, 1806.

28. Carte, plan et vue des bouches de Cataro et de la forteresse de Castel-novo occupes par les Russes en 1806. n.p., n. publ., n.d. Plate numbered "No. 14."

29. Carta delle provincie Illiriche co'loro diversi stabilimenti e con una parte degli stati limitrofi; compilata per ordine superiore nel deposito della guerra del regno d'Italia nell'anno MDCCCXIII. [Milan? Deposito della Guerra, 1813.]. Complete in 8 sheets. Sheets numbered to supplement the following map: Carta amministrativa del regno d'Italia co'suoi stabilimenti politici, militari, civili e religiosi e con una parte degli stati limitrofi . . . [Milan? Deposito della Guerra, 1813]. Scale: 1:500,000.

30. Koenigreich Illyrien nach der neuesten eintheilung. Prague, n. publ., 1825.

31. Kiepert, [Johann Samuel Heinrich]. Bosnien und Dalmatien; vorzueglich nach Osterreichischen Rufnahmen mit benutzung von A. Boues reisen (Montenegro nach Karaczay, Kowalewsky und Wilkinson, das untere Narenta thal nach Wilkinsons reise) Weimar, geographisches Institut, 1851. Scale: 1:800,000.

32. Kreis Cattaro. n.p. n. publ., [186–?].

33. Koenigreich Dalmatien, Glogau, C. Flemming. [1878?]. Scale: 1: 950,000. A copy of a map found in *Sohr-Berghaus hand-atlas ueber alle theile der erde neu bearbeitet von F. Handtke. Achte vermehrte und verbesserte auflage. Ausgabe in 100 blaettern nebst*

selbstaendigem ausfuehrlichen ortsverzeichniss. Glogau, Carl Fleming [187–?]. Map. no. 42.

34. Karta Tsrnogorske knjazhevine po najnovijem razgranichenju. [St. Petersburg, n. publ.] 1881. Complete in 4 sheets. Holdings: 3 sheets. Translation: Map of the principality of Montenegro according to the latest settlement of boundaries.

35. Handkte, F[riederich]. Bosnien, Herzegowina, Dalmatien und Montenegro. Glogau and Berlin, Carl Flemming, [187–?]. Scale: 1:600,000.

36. Walny's plan von Sarajevo und umgebung [Vienna], K[aiserlich] u[nd] k[oeniglich] militaer-geographisches institut, 1908. Scale: 1:10,000.

37. Uebersichts-karte von Bosnien und der Hercegovina. [Vienna], K[aiserlich] u[nd] k[oeniglich] militaer-geographisches institut, 1925. Scale: 1:750,000.

38. Sarajevo. [Washington], O[ffice of] s[trategic] s[ervices], 1943. Scale: 1:16,000.

39. S[ocialisticna] R[epublika] Bosna i Hercegovina. Zagreb, Ucila, 1968. Scale: 1:1,200,000.

40. Plan grada, Sarajeva, n.p. Voenogeografski institut, 1969. Scale not given.

41. S[ocialisticka] r[epublika] Bosna i Hercegovina. Zagreb, Izdanje "Tlos", 1976. Scale: 1:300,000. Complete in 2 sheets.

42. Sarajevo-Capajebo, 1986, plan grada . . . stadtplan, plan de la ville, plan of the town, la pianta della citta. Beograd, Geodetski zavod u Sarajevu, 1986. Scale: 1:20,000. Insets: Ilijas. Pale. Hadzici. Novo Sarajevo, Centar Sarajevo, Stari Grad.

43. NAP-LC

G	United States. Central Ingelligence Agency,
6844	Sarajevo and vicinity. Scale [ca. 1:250,00]. Vertical
.S2	exaggeration approx. 1:1 [Washington, D.C.?, Central
C19	Intelligence Agency, 1992]. 1 diagram : col.; on sheet
1992	26 × 36 cm. Computer-generated block diagram of
.U5	Sarajevo region drawn to resemble an aerial view. Relief shown by shading and spot heights Shipping list no.: 92-0577-P. Relief shown by shading and spot

north toward the upper left. Includes notes. "725715 (EO 0455) 7-92."
1. Block diagrams—Bosnia and Hercegovina—Sarajevo region.
2. Sarajevo region (Bosnia and Hercegovina)—Aerial views.
    I. Title

B. Maps of Bosnia, Herzegovina, or Sarajevo held by Various American Libraries

These records were retrieved from the maps file in the R.L.I.N. computerized catalog and then modified. Since these records were prepared by various libraries, their format varies. Most of the elements of each record are easily understood. However, two possibly unfamiliar elements—the ISBN (International Standard Book Number) and L.C. call number (Library of Congress call number) have been retained to help readers who may want to locate these maps on other automated library catalogs. Since almost all of these are very recent maps and likely to be used for tracking current developments, they have been listed in reverse chronological order.

1. Kümmerly + Frey. *Slowenien-Kroatien* = *Slovénie-Croatie* = *Slovenia-Croazia*. 1:500 000 / Kúmmerly + Frey. Scale 1:500,000 (E 13025_—E 19040_/N 47010_8N 41025_). Bern: Kümmerly + Frey, [1992?]. 1 map:col.; 126 × 91 cm. Road map with tourist features. Also covers most of Bosnia-Hercegovina. Relief shown by shading and spot heights. Legend in German, English, French, Italian, and Danish. Includes 2 insets. "W 08." ISBN 3259011110.
    1. Slovenia—Road maps. 2. Slovenia—Maps, Tourist. 3. Croatia—Road maps. 4. Croatia-Maps, Tourist. 5. Bosnia and Hercegovina—Road maps. 6. Bosnia and Hercegovina—Maps, Tourist.
    I. Title. II. Title: Slowenien-Kroatien 1:500 000. III. Title: Slowenien-Kroatien 1:500,000 L.C. Call No.: G6876.P2 1992 .K8.
2. United States. Central Intelligence Agency. *Newly independent*

Balkan states. Scale [ca. 1:3,168,000]. [Washington, D.C.: Central Intelligence Agency, 1992]. 1 map:col.; 17 × 17 cm. L.C. Call No.: G6801.A1 1992 .U5.

3. United States. Central Intelligence Agency. *Bosnia and Herzegovina.* Scale [ca. 1:2, 150,000] (E 150—E 200/N 460—N 420). [Washington, D.C.: Central Intelligence Agency, 1992]. 1 map:col.; 18 × 17 cm. L.C. Call No.: G6860 1992 .U5.

4. United States. Central Intelligence Agency. *Sarajevo and vicinity.* Scale [ca. 1:250,000]. Vertical exaggeration approx. 1:1. [Washington, D.C.: Central Intelligence Agency, 1992]. 1 diagram:col.; on sheet 26 × 36 cm. L.C. Call No.: G6844.S2C19 1992 .U5.

5. Eccopublic Trade (Firm). *Sarajevo, Jugoslavija*/design & realization, Eccopublic Trade, Sarajevo. English [ed.]. Scale not given. [Sarajevo, Bosnia and Hercegovina?: s.n., 1990?]. 1 map:col.; 29 × 43 cm., folded to 20 × 11 cm. L.C. Call No.: G6844.S2E635 1990. .E2 MLC.

6. Geodetski zavod u Sarajevu. Radna jedinica za kartografiju i reprodukciju karata. *Bjelašnica-Igman, planinarska karta:* 1:50 000 = Mountain map / Geodetski zavod u Sarajevu, Radna jedinica za kartografiju i reprodukciju karata. 1. izdanje. scale 1:50,000. Sarajevo [Bosnia and Hercegovina]: Planinarski savez Bosne i Hercegovine, 1987. 1 map:col.; 82 × 63 cm., folded to 23 × 11 cm. L.C. Call No.: G6862.B5E63 1987 .G4 MLC.

7. Bakšić, Mirsad. *Sarajevo 1986, plan grada* = [Sarajevo] 1986, [plan grada] = Stadtplan = Plan de la ville = *Plan of the town* = La pianta della citt'a / izradio, Geodetski zavod u Sarajevu, Radna jedinica za kartografiju i reprodukciju karata; autori, Bakšić Mirsad i Tomašević Branko. 3. dop. izdanje, juli 1986. Scale [ca. 1:20,000]. [Sarajevo, Bosnia and Hercegovina]: SOUR Svjetlost, OOUR Zavod za udžbenike i nastavna sredstva Sarajevo, [1986]. 1 map:col.; 64 × 75 cm., on sheet 69 × 100 cm., folded to 24 × 11 cm. L.C. Call No.: G6844.S2 1986 .B3 MLC.

8. Berann, Heinrich C. *XIV Olympic Winter Games Sarajevo 1984.* This *panorama* was painted for the official Olympic Committee Sarajevo by H. C. Berann. Not drawn to scale. [Sarajevo, Bosnia, and Hercegovina?]: The Committee, [1984]. 1 view:col.; 53 × 86 cm., on sheet 64 × 90 cm. L.C. Call No.: G6844.S2A3 1984 .B4.

9. Państwowe Przedsiębiorstwo Wydawnictw Kartograficznych. *Jugoslawia* / opracowanie Państwowego Przedsiębiorstwa Wydawnictw Kartograficznych-Warszawa. Wyd. 4. Scale 1:1,000,000 (E 130—E 240/N 470—N 400). Warszawa; Wroclaw: PPWK, 1983. 1 map:col.; 66 × 77 cm. (Mapa przeglądowa Europy). Series: Panstwowe Przedsiębiorstwo Wydawnictw Kartograficznych. Mapa przeglądowa Europy.

10. TLOS (Firm). OOUR Kartografija. *Bosna i Herzegovina* 1:500 000 / urednistvo, glavni urednik, prof. Zdravko Preclčec . . . [et al.]; izradeno u "TLOS" OOUR Kartografija-Zagreb. Scale 1:500,000 (E 15045_—E 19040_/N 45018_N 42025_). Zagreb [Croatia]: "TLOS" OOUR Kartografija, [1981] (Osijek [Croatia]: Litokarton, 1981). 1 map:col.; 69 × 69 cm., on sheet 71 × 98 cm., folded to 26 × 14 cm. L.C. Call No.: G6860 1981 .T5.

11. Geokarta (Firm). *Socijalistička Republika Bosna i Hercegovina*: razmjera 1:1 2500 00 / redaktor, Mara Živković. 8. izd. Scale 1:1,250,000 (E 140—E 210/N 460—N 420). Beograd: Zavod za kartografiju "Geokarta," 1978. 1 map:col.; 29 × 41 cm., folded to 33 × 23 cm. L.C. Call No.: G6861.C2 1978 .G4.

12. Mostar, Bosnia and Herzegovina. Uprava za turizam. *Mostar city plan* = Mostar Stadtplan / izdava_c, Uprava za turizam, Mostar. Mostar: Uprava za turizam, [1977?]. 1 map:col.; 21 × 29 cm. folded to 22 × 10 cm. L.C. Call No.: G6844.M6E635 1977 .M6.

13. Turistički savez Sarajevo. *Sarajevo, central pert* [sic] *of town* / published by Turistički savez Sarajevo. Sarajevo [Bosnia and Hercegovina]: Turistički savez, 1977. 1 map; on sheet 21 × 63 cm. folded to 21 × 11 cm. L.C. Call No.: G6844.S2E635 1977 .T8.

14. Tlos. *S. R. Bosna i Hercegovina*. Urednik: Zdravko Prelčec. 5. izdanje. Zagreb [Hrvatska] 1976. col. map 117 × 105 cm. on 2 sheets 69 × 113 cm. and 67 × 113 cm. L.C. Call No.: G6860 1976.T5.

15. Mišković, Milos D. *Karta razmjestaja stanovištva Socijalističke Republike Bosne i Hercegovina* / autor i redaktor dr. Miloš D. Milavsković. Scale 1:300,000 (E 15030_—E 19055_/N 45025_ —N 42020_). Sarajevo [Bosnia and Hercegovina]: Geografski institut prirodno-matematičkog fakulteta, 1976. 1 map on 4

sheets:col.; 119 × 124 cm., sheets 68 × 70 cm. or smaller. L.C. Call No.: G6861.E2 1971 .M5.

16. Geokarta (Firm). *Socijalistička Republika Bosna i Hercegovina* / izrada i reprodukcija "Geokarta" 1975; redaktor, Mara Živković. Beograd: Geokarta, [1975]. 1 map:col.; 31 × 42 cm. folded to 34 × 23 cm. L.C. Call No.: G6860 1975 .G4.

17. Bunardžić, Ratko. *Plan grada Sarajeva* / autor crteža, Ratko Bunardžić. [Beograd]: Vojnogeografski institut; Sarajevo: reklama i distribucija, Auto-moto savez BiH, 1973. 1 map:col.; 46 × 79 cm. folded in cover 22 × 12 cm. L.C. Call No.: G6844.S2 1973 .B8.

18. *Socialistička Republika Bosna i Hercegovina*. [Sarajevo? 1970?]. col. map 34 × 31 cm. L.C. Call No.: G6860 1970 .S6.

19. Učila, Zagreb. *SR Bosna i Hercegovina*. Zagreb [1970?]. col. map 29 × 43 cm. L.C. Call No.: G6860 1970 .U3.

20. Bunardžić, Ratko. *Plan grada Sarajeva*. [Beograd] Vojnogeografski institut; reklama i distribucija Auto-moto savez BiH, Sarajevo, 1969. col. map 46 × 79 cm. folded in cover 22 × 12 cm. L.C. Call No.: G6844.S2 1969 .B8.

21. Učila, Zabreb. *SR Bosna i Hercegovina*. Zagreb, 1968. col. map 29 × 43 cm. L.C. Call No.: G6860 1968 .U3.

22. Turistički savez Sarajevo. *Sarajevo* / published by Turistički savez Sarajevo. Scale not given. Sarajevo [Croatia]: Turistički savez, 1967. 1 map; on sheet 44 × 79 cm. folded in cover to 21 × 15 cm.

23. *Kroatien*. Scale not given.—[Germany? : s.n., 194–?] 1 map:photocopy; 65 × 67 cm. L.C. Call No.: G6871.F7 194– .K7 [War-time map, probably included some parts of Bosnia—ed.]

24. Waffen-SS. Abteilung Technische Wehrgeologie. *Wehrgeologische Karte des bosnisch-herzegowinisch-montenegrischen Grenzgebietes* / bearbeitet von der Abteilung Technische Wehrgeologie der Waffen-SS.—Sonderausgabe. Scale 1:200,000. 1 cm. = 2 km.—[Berlin?] : Hergestellt im Auftrage Gen. St. d. H. Abt. f. Kr. Kart. und Verm. Wes., [1939?–1945?] maps:col.; 56 × 41 cm.

25. *Generalna-Karta Bosne i Hercegovine*. Scale 1:600,000.—[S.l. : s.n.], 1919. 1 map:col.; 62 × 62 cm.

Index

This index lists almost all proper names of persons, places, and institutions (such as political parties). Also, an attempt has been made to include as wide a range of subjects as possible with special attention to those subjects that would not be in a historical work on another subject but that many readers of this work may look for—such as *ethnic cleansing*. In the interest of economy, for some subjects of considerable current interest, related words (such as *autonomous* and *autonomy*) have been grouped into one entry on the assumption that a reader interested in autonomy will be interested also in a reference to an autonomous entity. Also, different contributors, being more or less purist, used different spellings, more or less Latinized of various names and in some cases were insistent their spelling stand as is rather than be standardized. Accordingly, with a view to promoting peaceful coexistence, the varying spellings have been retained. When these sorted out right next to each other, as in the case of Abdul Hamid, proximity solves the problem. When a place has different names, an equal sign is followed by the more conventional name or form of the name in English.

The Editor